Unemployment Insurance Financing

Unemployment Insurance Financing

An Evaluation

Joseph M. Becker

American Enterprise Institute for Public Policy Research
Washington and London

Joseph M. Becker, S.J., is a professor at Georgetown University and a member of the Jesuit Center for Social Studies. He is vice-chairman of the Federal Advisory Council for Unemployment Insurance, in the Department of Labor, and has served as a consultant to the National Commission on Unemployment Compensation.

Library of Congress Cataloging in Publication Data

Becker, Joseph M.
    Unemployment insurance financing.

    (AEI studies ; 337)
    1. Insurance, Unemployment—United States—Finance.
I. Title.   II. Series.
HD7096.U5B432   368.4'4015'0973   81-15073
ISBN 0-8447-3462-4   AACR2
ISBN 0-8447-3463-2 (pbk.)

AEI Studies 337

Printed in the United States of America

Contents

List of Figures

Unemployment Insurance Financing

1
Time for Review

Forty-five years have elapsed since unemployment insurance was enacted, somewhat more than a generation. Those who prepared the original legislation have long since retired or died. It is time for a new generation living in an economy that has undergone many basic changes to ask whether the program we have inherited is still appropriate. Were the original choices wise? Are they still? Or is it time for something new?

This line of thought led the Federal Advisory Council to recommend the appointment of the National Commission on Unemployment Compensation (NCUC), and by 1980 the commission had completed its work. For its own good reasons, the commission accepted rather than reevaluated the original basic choices, taking as a given the fundamental structure. The commission concerned itself primarily with how to operate the program more effectively. It proceeded much as a congressional committee would, seeking specific solutions to immediate problems and relying more on public hearings than on basic research.

The approach that I shall take here is rather closer to that envisaged by the advisory council. I review two of the original basic decisions to ascertain whether they are still valid or should be reversed. One is the decision to make each state responsible for its own costs, the other, the decision to make each employer responsible for his own costs. Forty-five years of experience make reconsideration now a promising exercise. Whereas the original policy had to be made with hope guided by guesses, today's review finds a wealth of information available—still not as much as could be desired, but immensely more than in 1935.

Even if the results of our scrutiny reaffirm the original choices, the time spent in evaluation will not have been lost. Institutions run the risk of becoming obsolete, not simply because of changes in circumstance but also because their inheritors may no longer understand why the decisions were made initially. If basic insights are to remain vital and not atrophy, they must be recovered and renewed by each generation.

Scope of this Review

The unemployment insurance (UI) program has two parts, the inflow of taxes and the outflow of benefits. This review is confined to the first part, the financing of unemployment insurance. Financing is crucial, not only because it provides the funds needed for benefits, funds that have lately been in default, but even more because the method affects basic characteristics of the program. The deep, and sometimes bitter, differences of opinion about funding have their roots in the effects that the method of taxation is perceived to have on the inmost character of the program.

The evaluation of financing necessarily proceeds in terms of its two effects, the provision of adequate funds and the equitable distribution of the tax burden. The issue of adequacy is treated in chapter 2, and the issue of equity is treated in chapters 3, 4, and 5. Chapter 6, which deals with the taxable wage base, has implications for both adequacy and equity.

Except at the very beginning of unemployment insurance, the decision about the amount of funds to be raised has been derived, depending on prior judgments regarding the benefits to be paid. At the very beginning, when the country was in a deep depression and there was little information about the relation of benefit provisions to their cost, the principal determinant seems to have been the rate of tax that might safely be imposed; the states were expected to pay whatever benefits they could out of that tax.

Very soon thereafter, when unemployment benefits had become an accepted, almost irreversible, part of our national life, and when their cost was discovered to be much less than had been anticipated, the relationship was reversed. Ever since, the prior, and primary, decision has concerned the benefits to be paid, and taxes have been set accordingly. Except perhaps in a few states during a few years, the cost of unemployment benefits has never figured as importantly in the legislative process as the perceived value of the benefits. In most states, the chief reason that unemployment benefits are not more liberal is not that they cost so much but that they are not valued more highly. The reasons for this relative weighting are rooted in our nation's philosophy and history and include a preference for the competitive market as the main mechanism for distribution of income.[1]

---

[1] For further development of this proposition, see Joseph M. Becker, *Shared Government in Employment Security* (New York: Columbia University Press, 1959), chap. 1, and *Experience Rating in Unemployment Insurance* (Baltimore:

The second financing decision relates to the tax burden. Unlike determination of the amount, the decision about distribution is not derived but independent, stemming from the same fundamental social values that set the benefits themselves. This review will principally consider the distribution of the tax burden (chapters 3 through 6).

Historically, the distribution of the tax burden has involved two major decisions. The first regulated apportionment among the states, and the second, among employers. The first question was whether to make each state responsible for its own costs or, alternatively, to pool all costs by means of a uniform national tax. Second was the matter of whether to make each employer responsible for his own costs or to pool costs among all employers—within a state or within the nation.

Preference for Individual Responsibility

Until the present, the preponderant choice of our society has been the first alternative in each case—to place the responsibility on each state and, within each state, on each employer.[2] Both choices are the fruits of an American trait that for want of a better term may be called "individualism"—the tendency to give the benefit of the doubt to the individualistic side of the dynamic tension depicted in figure 1. Persons living in a group must continually choose between individual and group responsibility as the mechanism for solving problems that affect the members of the group. Road building may be made the task of the group, whereas the provision of an automobile may be left to the individual.

The two poles of the tension represent alternatives: A move toward one means a move away from the other. The tension is dynamic: Every living agent consists of a bundle of dynamic tensions that energize its activity. The tension is dynamic also in the sense that the balance point between the poles is constantly shifting—now toward one pole, now toward the other. That is why the axis connecting the poles is depicted with an arrow at either end. The flow of vital energy surges back and forth. The societies of the Soviet Union and of the United States differ primarily in the balance they

Johns Hopkins University Press, 1972), chap. 1. The reasons also include apprehension about something vaguely called "abuse"; see Joseph M. Becker, S.J., *The Problem of Abuse in Unemployment Benefits* (New York: Columbia University Press, 1953), chap. 2.

[2] There was an early Missouri plan that went even further in the direction of individual responsibility: it would have established a reserve for each employee, a kind of personal savings account.

FIGURE 1
THE NATION'S VALUES

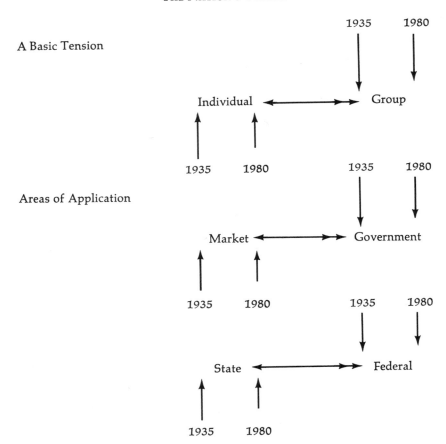

SOURCE: Author.

have established between the individual and the group, especially the group called the sovereign state.

The horizontal axis connecting "individual" and "group" is depicted with a double arrow pointing toward "group." This represents the common judgment among social historians that during the last half century the balance point in this country has been moving in the direction of the group. Our society currently relies more on group responsibility than it did fifty years ago. The enactment of the unemployment insurance law itself was a move in the direction of group responsibility. Before 1935 the support of the unemployed worker was almost entirely the responsibility of the individual and his family; after 1935 much of this task became the responsibility of the large group called government.

The vertical arrows on the diagram have a different significance. Unlike the horizontal arrows, which are historical statements, the vertical arrows are ethical statements. They indicate that one alternative is given an antecedent preference over the other. As it is drawn, the chart represents a judgment, widely shared, that in 1935 the preference of the American society was for individual responsibility. The history of the enactment of unemployment insurance itself amply indicates the uphill struggle that was required to prevail against this strong early preference.

As used here, the term "preference" means that the preferred option enjoys the benefit of the doubt, whereas the burden of proof rests on the alternative option. The arrows pointing up—in a supportive position, as it were—indicate the option that enjoys the benefit of the doubt. The downward-pointing arrows indicate the option that must be proved. The length of the respective lines reflects the intensity of the preference.

The allocation of the burden of proof is of great significance, probably more so than any other single factor. This is because in the social sciences, as contrasted with physical and mathematical fields, compelling proof is difficult, sometimes impossible, to obtain. For this reason, the alternative that enjoys the benefit of the doubt has a great advantage. Whenever clear evidence is lacking—the more frequent situation—the favored alternative wins by default.

When the justices of the United States Supreme Court voted on the constitutionality of unemployment insurance, their vote was four to four in the first case and five to four in the second. Yet they all worked with the same evidence. The difference in the votes can probably be explained largely by their differing preferences for individual and group responsibility, that is, on the placement and length of their vertical lines.

It is rare even in the case of the academician that there are no vertical lines at work. In the case of the decision maker, an additional factor is operative. The decision maker *must* have antecedent preferences if he is to function effectively. Without the operation of the vertical arrows, the decision maker will sometimes find it impossible to arrive at a decision. This is because clear evidence is often lacking for either side. Without first knowing which side must bear the burden of producing proof, the decision maker would logically be unable to function. Still, in all circumstances, he must make a decision. Hence the necessity of the vertical arrows.

The basic tension between the individual and the group affects many areas of human life and produces "subtensions." Two subtensions particularly relevant to unemployment insurance are illustrated in figure 1, that between the government and the market and that between the federal and state governments. The lines have the same meaning as in the basic tension between group and individual. These subtensions express the central issues involved in the decisions that are the object of the present review—the judgments that make each employer and state responsible for their own costs.

Source of Preference

The vertical lines accord the benefit of the doubt to individual action while placing the burden of proof on group action. This was certainly true in 1935; it was still true in 1980, although less so. Here the important aspect of the vertical lines is their source—fear of a too-pervasive government, which of course led the founding fathers to devise our elaborate system of governmental checks and balances.

One of the more accurate and eloquent explanations of that fear was written by a visitor. It was in 1830 that Alexis de Tocqueville came to the United States and wrote his classic *Democracy in America*. At that time he found a country uniquely devoted to individual wants as opposed to collective needs. Tocqueville saw this individualism as a natural product of the democratic quality of American life. Unlike aristocratic societies, in which everyone belongs to a social class that goes far to establish his perception of himself, in the American democracy the citizens saw themselves as all equal, an undifferentiated mass of identical units, each one of which was significant in its own right: "They owe nothing to any man, they expect nothing from any man; they acquire the habit of always considering themselves as standing alone, and they are apt to imagine that their whole destiny is in their own hands."[3]

Despite his perception of the individualistic bent of American society, Tocqueville was deeply concerned with the threat of a future despotism. He predicted that government in America would grow greatly in both scope and size and would become more centralized.[4] He based his view on the nature of a modern democracy. First of all, in a democracy subjects are willing to grant a ruler great power because they consider that government is their creation; when they

[3] Alexis de Tocqueville, *Democracy in America*, vol. 2 (New York: Vintage Books, 1954), p. 105.
[4] Ibid., pp. 311-12.

obey it, they are in a sense only obeying themselves. Second, in a democracy equality ranks high in the hierarchy of social values. Yet equality is extraordinarily difficult to achieve. To many citizens the most direct route to equality will seem to be to give everybody the same amount of influence (one vote) and then to concentrate all power in government. Third, whether or not the first two forces are operative, competition between citizens for favors will constantly augment government's power. In Tocqueville's words:

> It frequently happens that the members of the community promote the influence of the central power without intending to. . . . [They] will admit, as a general principle, that the public authority ought not to interfere in private concerns; but, by an exception to that rule, each of them craves its assistance in the particular concern on which he is engaged and seeks to draw upon the influence of the government for his own benefit, although he would restrict it on all other occasions. If a large number of men applies this particular exception to a great variety of different purposes, the sphere of the central power extends itself imperceptibly in all directions, although everyone wishes it to be circumscribed. Thus a democratic government increases its power simply by the fact of its permanence. Time is on its side; every incident befriends it; the passions of individuals unconsciously promote it; and it may be asserted that the older a democratic community is, the more centralized will its government become.[5]

Tocqueville's concern found an echo in 1911, when Great Britain enacted the world's first unemployment insurance law. The English historian Hilaire Belloc used the occasion to write *The Servile State*, in which he argued that unemployment insurance was the beginning of a trend toward a "servile state" in which the government would perform the role of a benevolent but all-powerful parent. In the 1920s, in the United States, Samuel Gompers led the American Federation of Labor in opposition to all proposals for government-provided unemployment benefits precisely because he feared the emergence of the servile state. "What the government gives," he repeatedly argued, "the government can take away."

The fear of Tocqueville's benevolent despotism and Belloc's servile state blocked all proposals for unemployment insurance in the

[5] Ibid., p. 306. George Stigler and Sam Peltzman, both of the University of Chicago, have been giving this simple, central notion a formal economic expression with respect to governmental regulation of economic agents. See articles published in the *Bell Journal of Economics* covering the period 1971 through 1977.

United States for a quarter of a century after its inauguration in England. The vertical lines were so long that the burden of proof was heavy indeed. Nevertheless, many competent people were at work producing the required proof.[6] Among those in this country, in the 1920s, were members of the Wisconsin school, such as John R. Commons, John B. Andrews and his American Association for Labor Legislation, Paul Raushenbush with his wife, Elizabeth Brandeis, and many others. Also at work were members of the Ohio school, such as Isaac Rubinow and Paul Douglas, and many others. A detailed history of the early attempts to enact compulsory unemployment insurance is available in a number of sources and need not be given here.[7]

Original Decisions

Wisconsin enacted the first unemployment insurance law in January 1932, almost three years before the national Social Security Act of 1935. The Wisconsin approach was individualistic and market oriented from the beginning—as in the Huber Bill of 1921, which pooled reserves but taxed only employers and experience-rated the tax. (Most of the laws that the states eventually enacted were—and still are—similar in their financing provisions to this earliest Wisconsin bill rather than to the law that Wisconsin finally enacted.) The market orientation was strengthened in successive bills submitted to the Wisconsin legislature as experience with the legislature proved the necessity of moving as far as possible from anything resembling welfare.

It was the most individualistic of the plans, the Groves Bill, providing for separate employer reserves, that was finally—and barely—pushed through the Wisconsin legislature in 1931 and signed in January 1932. No other plan in any state was enacted. Histories of that early period generally fail to accord full recognition to the difference between a law (as in Wisconsin) and a plan (as in other

[6] In England one of the early voices was that of William Beveridge, who published his influential work *Unemployment: A Problem of Industry* in 1910.

[7] Daniel Nelson, *Unemployment Insurance: The American Experience, 1915-1935* (Madison: University of Wisconsin Press, 1969); Roy Lubove, *The Struggle for Social Security, 1900-1935* (Cambridge, Mass.: Harvard University Press, 1968); Edwin E. Witte, "Development of Unemployment Compensation," *Yale Law Journal*, vol. 55, no. 1 (December 1945); Arthur J. Altmeyer, *The Formative Years of Social Security* (Madison: University of Wisconsin Press, 1966); Paul A. Raushenbush and Elizabeth Brandeis Raushenbush, *Our "U.C." Story (1930-1967)* (Madison, Wis.: privately published, May 1978); and William Haber and Merrill G. Murray, *Unemployment Insurance in the American Economy* (Homewood, Ill.: Richard D. Irwin, 1966).

states). That is, writers fail to recognize the extreme length of the vertical arrows at that time and the extent to which enactment into law required that a plan be individualistic. It was not until the fall of 1932, half a year after the enactment of the Wisconsin law, that the American Federation of Labor changed its stand from opposition to approval of compulsory unemployment insurance.

An impressive body of evidence gradually accumulated indicating that in the modern economy the average worker could not adequately protect himself against the threat of unemployment. As a result, opposition to an unemployment insurance program gradually lessened. The Great Depression swept away enough of the remaining opposition to allow the enactment of the Social Security Act and the construction of the unemployment insurance system that has functioned for nearly half a century. It is this program that we shall review here, a program not as individualistic as the original Wisconsin law of 1932 but not as communitarian as some of the alternative plans considered by Congress and by the states before they made their final decisions. In the end, Congress settled financial responsibility principally on the individual states, and the states settled financial responsibility principally on the individual employer.

Both of these decisions had the strong backing of President Roosevelt. According to Arthur Altmeyer, the president's choice of a federal/state system over a single national system stemmed from his basic political philosophy.

> The President's desire to rely upon the states as much as possible was based upon his lifelong belief in our federal form, rather than a national form, of government. This conviction antedated his experience as a state senator and governor. It can be traced back to the influence of the great British Ambassador, James Lord Bryce, whom he knew personally and whose book *The American Commonwealth*, had impressed him deeply. He was particularly interested in Bryce's thesis that a major advantage of our federal system was the opportunity it afforded for the individual states to serve as laboratories.[8]

The president also threw his weight on the side of individualism by the support he gave experience rating.[9]

Since 1935, there have been changes in the horizontal and vertical lines of figure 1. In the two subtensions that are the particular concern of this review, the horizontal balance point has shifted

[8] Altmeyer, *Formative Years*, p. 11.
[9] Witte, "Development," p. 75.

9

(hence the double arrows) toward the "group" pole. Whether it is measured by number of employees or by expenditures, government has grown faster than the private sector during the life of the nation.[10] Within government, the federal influence over the states has greatly increased.[11] These horizontal shifts are partially (in my judgment, principally) explained by the accumulation of evidence that the individual is unable to do what needs to be done. They are explained, also, by the process that Tocqueville foresaw and that everyone now recognizes in its fulfillment—a steady stream of requests by citizens for governmental favors. In addition, there has been the development analyzed by John Maurice Clark: Organized private groups have grown so powerful that government has had to grow to control them.[12]

The horizontal shift may be partially explained also by changes in the vertical lines, that is, by switches in values. The vertical lines may be shorter in 1980 than they were in 1935. Nevertheless, their position is still the same—with the free market preferred to government control and state autonomy preferred to federal control, all other things being equal. Some support for that judgment is found in various polls. For example, in 1976 Lou Harris surveyed 150 leading colleges and found that they preferred corporate to government giving by 72 percent to 16 percent. Again, in several polls in recent years, respondents have favored state over federal action, expressing specific judgment that the states are closer to the actual problems and are less wasteful. In 1978 Gallup conducted a poll that asked the question: "Which in your judgment poses the greatest future threat to the country?" The answers were:

- Government: 47 percent
- Labor: 19 percent
- Business: 19 percent
- Don't know: 15 percent

[10] A recent study covering the period 1792-1974 compared the growth of taxes with the growth of total economic activity and compared the growth of public employment with the growth of the total labor force. The rate of growth of the public sector has always been greater than that of the private sector, the largest difference occurring during the period 1929-1951. Overall, the public sector has grown almost twice as fast as the private. See Allen H. Meltzer and Scott F. Richard, "Why Government Grows in a Democracy," *Public Interest* (Summer 1978).

[11] To cite one example, federal aid as a percentage of total state-local revenues increased from 8 percent in 1954 to 20 percent in 1976. See Advisory Commission on Intergovernmental Relations, *In Brief* (Washington, D.C., 1978), a twenty-seven-page summary of fourteen volumes published.

[12] John M. Clark, *Alternative to Serfdom* (New York: Alfred A. Knopf, 1950).

10

In a national survey of American professors, 81 percent agreed that "the private business system in the United States, for all its flaws, works better than any other system devised for advanced industrial societies."[13] Additional support for the view that the vertical lines of 1935 are still in place is found in the fact that Congress has not (yet) fused the fifty-one separate state programs into one national program, and the states have not (yet) added government or employee contributions to the employer tax, nor have they (yet) forsaken the experience-rating feature of the employer tax.

The 1980 elections reflected a shift along the horizontal axis back toward individual responsibility, a change clearly caused by a lengthening of the vertical value lines. How profound or long lasting the latest shift will be remains to be seen. It suffices, however, to establish that the principle of subsidiarity is still an applicable tool in the task of reevaluating unemployment insurance. The principle of subsidiarity states that wherever possible the smaller unit of society is to be given preference over the larger in the assignment of social functions and that the larger unit is to give help (*subsidium*) to the smaller so that the smaller unit can better perform its proper function. When there is a function to be allocated, the smaller unit thus enjoys the benefit of the doubt, whereas the larger must carry the burden of proof.

To one who accepts the principle of subsidiarity, as I do, the process of reevaluation becomes a matter of examining forty-five years' experience to see if there is clear evidence that the original choices were or are unwise. Only clear evidence will supply the proof required by the principle of subsidiarity.

Two principal decisions reviewed here are: (1) the decision to make each state responsible for its own costs and (2) the decision, within each state, to make each employer responsible for his own costs. Should these original decisions be changed now or reconfirmed? The choice is, as always, difficult but inevitable, and this review will, I hope, be of some assistance.[14] At the end, there will remain areas where the evidence is not compelling. At that point, the location of the vertical arrows may be decisive, for a choice must still be made.

[13] Everett C. Ladd and Seymour M. Lipset, "Professors Found to Be Liberal but Not Radical," *Chronicle of Higher Education*, January 16, 1978, p. 18.

[14] In this review, I have not hesitated to draw on earlier writings of my own because my purpose has been less to introduce new issues than to revive the old, basic issues and to gather together all that is pertinent to their reevaluation.

2
State Responsibility for Solvency

In the organization of any society, a basic decision involves the degree of centralization in the structure of government. This was the principal issue in the debate between Hamilton and Jefferson. Hamilton sought to concentrate power in the federal government; Jefferson sought to diffuse it. The decision to make each state primarily responsible for its own unemployment insurance program and for its own costs was Jeffersonian. The story of this decision, which did not come easily, has been told many times and need not be repeated here.[1] The wisdom of the decision, however, does need to be reevaluated from time to time in the light of actual performance by the states.

The first measure of a financial system is, of course, the effect exerted on financing itself. The principal norms are, as usual, adequacy and equity. In this context adequacy relates to the total amount of taxes collected and tends to take the form of a discussion of "solvency"; equity relates to the distribution of the tax burden and tends to take the form of a discussion of "cost sharing."

Discussion here is limited, as usual, to the operations of the regular UI program, that is, to the payment of benefits for twenty-six, possibly thirty-nine, weeks. Beyond these limits lies the very different world of the long-term unemployed, for whom adequacy and equity both take on different meanings and are to be judged by different norms. This chapter is limited to the issue of adequacy, or solvency. The issue of equity is taken up in the following chapters.

For a number of reasons solvency was an important concern of the planners when unemployment insurance was inaugurated. First of all, the costs of the program were very uncertain. Without previous experience, cost estimates had to be largely guesswork. For

[1] See especially Daniel Nelson, *Unemployment Insurance: The American Experience, 1915-1935* (Madison: University of Wisconsin Press, 1969); Edwin E. Witte, *The Development of the Social Security Act* (Madison: University of Wisconsin Press, 1962); and Paul A. Raushenbush and Elizabeth Brandeis Raushenbush, *Our "U.C." Story (1930-1967)* (Madison, Wis.; privately published, May 1978).

example, an early plan included a uniform tax of 5 percent on total payrolls—about five times the actual cost of a program much more liberal than the one then contemplated.

Second, the planners were concerned to make this program one of "insurance," by which they meant primarily a program free of the taint of relief. It was judged essential for the program to be self-supporting and for the beneficiaries to be able to say that they had earned their benefits. President Roosevelt emphasized this aspect of the program above all others in his addresses to the nation and to Congress.

Third, England's experience with its unemployment insurance program in the 1920s was still fresh in everyone's mind. After the British unemployment insurance fund was exhausted, benefits were continued through an infusion of general revenues by one emergency act after another. The British "dole" was very much in the forefront of the discussion of social security in this country, and all the friends of unemployment insurance wanted confirmation that the American system would not experience the same bankruptcy.

Finally, the concept of deficit financing was still new and not very salable to the general public. Franklin D. Roosevelt in his first presidential campaign vigorously attacked the "spendthrift Hoover" and promised to cut government expenses if elected. The real lesson of the British experience was not then clear—that even the very large debts of the unemployment insurance system could and would be paid off in the ensuing periods of prosperity.

National Experience

The states' record in maintaining solvency is to be judged by the answers to two questions: (1) Were the funds always available to pay the covenanted benefits? and (2) Was this end attained in a manner appropriate to a social insurance program?

The answer to the first question is clear enough: All legitimate claims in all the states have always been paid.[2] One reason for this successful record is simply that the unemployment insurance tax represents a relatively small burden. The cost for the country as a whole has averaged only 1.2 percent of total wages and, except for Alaska, did not reach 2 percent in any state (see figure 2). True, the

[2] Except that in Alaska, in one year, benefit payments were held up for a brief period for lack of funds. Although Wisconsin provided for individual employer reserves in its original law, it never actually had to deny benefits to individual claimants because in 1935 it added a common account out of which benefits could be paid to any claimant whose employer's individual account was exhausted.

FIGURE 2

BENEFIT-COST RATES, BY STATE, CUMULATIVE 1940–1978

Rank and state	Total payroll (in thousands)	Cost rate (percentage of total payroll)
All states	$10,221,008,702	1.198
1. Alaska	21,695,691	2.718
2. Rhode Island	48,282,871	1.909
3. New Jersey	411,063,792	1.674
4. Idaho	26,903,663	1.650
5. California	1,088,603,272	1.628
6. Washington	167,838,736	1.625
7. Nevada	29,842,340	1.614
8. Massachusetts	329,247,154	1.545
9. Vermont	14,138,356	1.544
10. Oregon	105,922,066	1.487
11. Maine	38,542,349	1.475
12. Pennsylvania	672,086,257	1.401
13. Connecticut	195,548,983	1.398
14. North Dakota	15,806,986	1.362
15. Hawaii	36,620,732	1.357
16. Wyoming	15,376,999	1.352
17. Kentucky	111,489,985	1.352
18. Michigan	545,555,429	1.346
19. New York	1,175,337,605	1.327
20. Montana	24,845,514	1.284
21. Mississippi	58,251,907	1.283
22. New Hampshire	32,539,138	1.209
23. Kansas	83,059,882	1.197
24. Wisconsin	222,912,739	1.191
25. Tennessee	155,879,982	1.179
26. Louisiana	139,905,249	1.145
27. Arkansas	58,229,682	1.141
28. North Carolina	199,611,654	1.135
29. Utah	42,847,515	1.132
30. New Mexico	33,848,158	1.101
31. West Virginia	80,393,980	1.093
32. South Carolina	93,070,017	1.080
33. Alabama	119,254,397	1.048
34. Arizona	73,382,024	1.032
35. Delaware	34,229,671	1.024
36. Georgia	180,701,904	1.017
37. Minnesota	182,044,552	1.016
38. Maryland	169,359,972	1.013
39. Illinois	697,765,476	.962
40. Missouri	227,019,479	.935
41. Ohio	631,692,449	.893
42. Nebraska	53,170,840	.859
43. Oklahoma	93,332,619	.855
44. Iowa	108,002,501	.852
45. District of Columbia	59,788,770	.846
46. Indiana	280,288,426	.841
47. Florida	267,090,411	.777
48. South Dakota	16,203,998	.776
49. Colorado	97,779,855	.705
50. Virginia	171,452,654	.580
51. Texas	480,150,021	.484

NOTE: Cumulative total of benefits paid plus benefit reserves, as percentage of cumulative total covered payroll. Data, from U.S. Department of Labor, based on tabulations by state agencies, may not add because of rounding.

a Excludes data for Puerto Rico.

SOURCE: Division of Research and Statistics, Ohio Bureau of Employment Services, Columbus.

cost has been rising, but even now the unemployment insurance tax is less than a fifth of the other social insurance tax (Old-Age, Survivors, Disability, and Health Insurance, or OASDHI), less than a twentieth of all fringe benefits, and a very tiny fraction of all production costs. This relative size of the unemployment insurance tax must be kept in mind in the discussion of every issue of unemployment insurance financing.

Another reason is that deficit financing has become a recognized tool of government. In contrast to the period before the Keynesian revolution, it is now acceptable for government, especially the federal government, to borrow in order to meet current needs. Explicit provision for state borrowing was made as early as 1944 with a view to guarding against the anticipated unemployment of the reconversion period. Provision for the infusion of general revenues was made in 1954, by the Reed Act. Given the ability and willingness of the state and federal governments to borrow, the payment of benefits is as assured as any payment can be.

The answer to the second question—whether the states conducted their affairs in a manner appropriate to an "insurance" program—requires more analysis. The answer depends on (1) how successful the states were in repaying their loans, (2) how infrequently they resorted to borrowing, and (3) their justification for borrowing at all.

The first condition is, of course, the essential one. Failure on the part of the states to pay their debts could easily bring basic changes to the present federal/state relationship. On the other hand, if borrowing states always repay—as they must under existing law—the principle that each state is responsible for its own costs remains inviolate. Buying on credit, if followed by repayment, is a normal business practice that carries no stigma.

Nevertheless, the second consideration is important. "Insurance" normally supposes the prepayment of funds from which benefits are later drawn. Involved here is the impalpable but very significant element of public image. The spectacle of twenty-five states "going broke" tarnishes the reputation of the program in the minds of the public, most of whom are not professional economists accustomed to deficit financing.

Furthermore, since the loans are interest free, they automatically provide a subsidy to the states receiving them. To this extent it becomes less true that each state bears its own costs. Inflation automatically increases the subsidy. Finally, when taxes are postponed, they affect a cohort of employers different from that which would be affected if they were levied closer to the time the benefit costs were incurred. Some of the firms responsible for the unemployment of the 1970s will not be available for taxation in later years. Deficit financing thus undercuts another principle of the system, that within each state each employer should be responsible for his own costs.

The importance of the third criterion for judging the performance of the states is obvious. To the extent that the states were justified in borrowing, their reputation for responsibility—presuming repayment of the loans—remains essentially unscathed. To the extent that the borrowing was not justified but was due to obvious faults on the part of the states, there is reason to consider changes in the financial structure of the program so as to rely less on state responsibility.

To assess the states' record in these three respects, a brief review of solvency history is useful. The essential elements in that history are the inflow to the fund (employer taxes), the outflow (benefits paid), and the reserve remaining. Table 1 shows this history by year, for all states combined, from 1938 through 1978, the latest year for which data were available. Benefits, taxes, and reserves are all shown as percentages of total wages in covered employment. By thus expressing all items as rates, we may follow developments over time without the distortions that changes in coverage, wages, and benefits impose on measures expressed in dollar amounts. Rates also facilitate comparisons between states.

After 1938, a recession year, the benefit-cost rate began to decline and during the war years (1941–1944) dropped very rapidly indeed. In 1944, less than 0.1 percent of wages was paid out in benefits. Tax rates also declined, but not as fast as cost rates. As a result, the reserve funds for the system as a whole grew steadily until 1945, when they peaked at over 10 percent of payrolls. For most states this represented considerable overfunding.

Hence the states acted to lower taxes. The average tax rate declined steadily until the 1949–1950 recession, after which it rose only briefly before continuing its long descent. As a result, the reserve ratio (reserve as a percentage of wages) fell without interruption from 1945 until 1962; thereafter it stabilized during the prosperous years of the late 1960s at about 3.0–3.5. This seems to have represented the amount of reserves that the states at that time were willing to hold—not much more, not much less. The explanation is not that the states were unable to pay more for unemployment insurance but rather that they were simply unwilling to hold larger reserves.

Then came the 1970s, when the reserve ratio dropped to unprecedented lows. The drop was caused partly by an increase in the benefit burden, but this was not the entire, or even the chief, explanation. The system had successfully surmounted higher benefit costs

TABLE 1

Benefits, Taxes, and Reserves as a Percentage of Total Wages: U.S. Totals, 1938–1978

Year	Benefits	Taxes	Reserves	Year	Benefits	Taxes	Reserves
1938	2.11	2.69	4.24	1959	1.22	1.05	3.69
1939	1.55	2.66	5.29	1960	1.40	1.17	3.41
1940	1.60	2.50	5.60	1961	1.72	1.23	2.91
1941	0.82	2.37	5.99	1962	1.23	1.39	2.95
1942	0.63	1.98	6.18	1963	1.24	1.35	2.98
1943	0.12	1.86	7.13	1964	1.05	1.27	3.05
1944	0.09	1.67	8.78	1965	0.84	1.18	3.24
1945	0.67	1.50	10.37	1966	0.62	1.07	3.46
1946	1.49	1.24	9.35	1967	0.69	0.89	3.57
1947	0.90	1.19	8.43	1968	0.61	0.77	3.54
1948	0.82	1.01	7.91	1969	0.58	0.70	3.46
1949	1.85	1.07	7.47	1970	1.01	0.66	3.11
1950	1.33	1.18	6.76	1971	1.23	0.65	2.40
1951	0.71	1.20	6.56	1972	0.98	0.85	2.06
1952	0.78	1.08	6.52	1973	0.79	0.98	2.15
1953	0.69	0.93	6.41	1974	1.07	0.94	1.90
1954	1.48	0.79	6.00	1975	2.03	0.90	0.53
1955	0.91	0.81	5.56	1976	1.39	1.16	0.13
1956	0.84	0.88	5.21	1977	1.16	1.29	0.13
1957	1.00	0.85	4.99	1978	0.93	1.37	0.55
1958	2.05	0.86	4.05				

Source: U.S. Department of Labor, *Handbook of Unemployment Insurance Financial Data, 1938-1978.*

in an earlier period: Benefit costs had averaged 1.44 during 1957–1962, as compared with 1.28 during 1970–1976 (table 17). The difference in the reserve ratios of the two periods is explained chiefly by a pair of other factors.

First, at the beginning of the earlier period, some of the excessive reserves inherited from the war were still available; second, during that earlier period the average tax rate was maintained at a higher level (1.10 as compared with 0.88). In the 1970s, on the contrary, after starting with a lesser backlog, the states maintained a lower tax rate.

As a result, when the second, and unusually long, recession of the 1970s struck the states, twenty-five jurisdictions were forced to borrow. Table 19 shows these jurisdictions and their borrowing history as of the end of 1978. (The end of 1978 is a convenient point at which to take stock of the system's recuperative powers. Recovery from the 1974–1975 recession would have been in progress by this time, and the finances of the program should have begun to show improvement.) Such widespread insolvency inevitably raises the question of state capability. How is such a collapse to be evaluated? Is it a sign of some permanent weakness calling for a basic restructuring of the financial mechanism, perhaps with more federal participation, or is the recent experience traceable to exceptional and temporary circumstances that the system may be expected to overcome with its present structure?

Certainly the states cannot claim that they were caught by surprise. They had been given a preview in the 1950s, when the program was required to weather two severe recessions in close succession. Indeed, this experience led to the development of an early warning signal, the "reserve multiple." This measure was developed in the aftermath of the 1958 recession, when several states were forced to borrow and many more saw their reserves depleted to a dangerous level. The Interstate Conference of Employment Security Agencies (ICESA) charged its Benefit Financing Committee with the task of developing guidelines for use by the states in maintaining solvency.

In a substantial report published in September 1959, this committee developed the "reserve multiple" and recommended its use by the states. The reserve multiple is the ratio between two other ratios, between reserves (expressed as a percentage of total wages) and a state's highest twelve-month benefit-cost ratio (also expressed as a percentage of total wages). Thus expressed, the standard automatically reflects changes in wage, employment, and benefit levels and thus provides a more accurate guide to future costs than the measures expressed in terms of taxable wages or, worst of all, some fixed dollar amount. Although the committee recognized that no one measure would prove adequate for all states under all circumstances, it proposed the reserve multiple as the most promising.

The ICESA committee recommended that a state maintain a reserve multiple in the range of 1.5 to 3.0, depending on each state's particular situation. As was to be expected, the attention of the states, like that of the federal government, has tended to center on the minimum ratio of 1.5. A state with this reserve multiple would be capable of paying benefits, without any further tax revenue, for one and one-half years at the highest annual cost rate ever previously experienced. A reserve below this level was to be considered inadequate short of proof to the contrary.

The recent recession was a test of the usefulness of this solvency standard. At the beginning of the 1970s, after the long period of prosperity in the 1960s, when reserves should have been at their maximum, thirty-six of the fifty-two jurisdictions had reserves that met the 1.5 norm, whereas sixteen did not. Of the thirty-six with "adequate" reserves, twenty-five, or 69 percent, survived the 1970s without having to borrow. Of the sixteen with "inadequate" reserves, only three, or 19 percent, escaped borrowing. We may look at the same picture in reverse: Whereas 81 percent of the states with inadequate reserves had to borrow, only 31 percent of the states with adequate reserves borrowed.

It would seem that the minimum reserve multiple of 1.5 provides a useful measure of the likelihood that a state will remain solvent. On the other hand, this norm is not infallible. Of the thirty-six states with adequate reserves, eleven nevertheless had to borrow. Also, three of the states with inadequate reserves weathered the recession without borrowing. Table 2 shows the reserve multiples of twenty-four jurisdictions, omitting the Virgin Islands, that were forced to borrow during the recent recession. They are about equally divided between those with and those without adequate reserves: At the start of the 1970s eleven had adequate reserves, and thirteen did not.

Of the thirteen borrowing states with inadequate reserves, the question might be asked: How many would have escaped insolvency if they had started the 1970s with reserves adequate by the 1.5 norm? The answer is: only two—Nevada and Ohio.[3] Two other states would have been helped substantially, however, if they had started the 1970s with a reserve multiple of at least 1.5. Michigan's debt would have been cut by 75 percent, and Montana's by 71 percent. On the average, the debt of states with inadequate reserves would have been cut by 25 percent if they had met the minimum standard. (See table 20.) In the light of the experience of the 1970s, it must be concluded that the minimum of the recommended range (1.5 to 3.0) is not a safe solvency criterion for many states.

In retrospect, it seems clear that the states should have built their reserves higher during the prosperous period of 1963–1969. Why did they not do so? A number of factors enter into the explanation, some technical, some political. First, the long preceding period of excessive reserves had engendered a feeling of security whose basis eroded so gradually that it escaped notice. Although the reserve ratio sank steadily for sixteen years, the drop was slow and received

[3] Ohio's fund was not actually exhausted at this time. As the fund approached exhaustion, the state made a precautionary application for a loan of $1.9 million, which was granted. This loan, however, was not actually needed and was never paid.

TABLE 2

Date of First Loan, Debts, Reserve Multiple, and Selected Benefit Provisions for Borrowing States

	Date of First Loan (1)	Debts (end of 1978)			Reserve Multiple[b] (end of 1969) (5)	Benefit Provisions[c] (1978) (6)
		Amount ($ thousands) (2)	Percentage of total wages[a] (3)	Rank by (3) (4)		
Alabama	12/75	27,000	0.28	17	1.66	1
Arkansas	1/76	19,500	0.40	16	1.46	(1)
Connecticut	3/72	410,497	3.39	3	1.41	1 –2–3–4
Delaware	11/75	47,000	2.07	8	1.22	1 –4
District of Columbia	11/75	64,473	1.86	9	4.57	(1) –3–4
Florida	4/76	DR		—	2.42	(1)
Hawaii	1/76	DR		—	1.79	(1)–2 –4
Illinois	12/75	946,500	2.09	7	1.17	(1)–2–3–4
Maine	9/75	36,400	1.42	11	1.23	1 –3–4
Maryland	3/76	DR		—	1.73	1 –2–3
Massachusetts	4/75	265,000	1.38	12	1.74	(1) –3–4

		[a]	[b]				[c]
Michigan	4/75	624,000	1.70	10	0.85		1 –3
Minnesota	7/75	172,000	1.32	13	1.11		(1) –4
Montana	4/76	10,484	0.60	14	1.16		(1) –4
Nevada	1/76	DR	—	—	1.26		1 –4
New Jersey	1/75	694,928	2.61	6	1.22		(1) –4
New York	2/77	335,750	0.52	15		1.91	(1)–2
Ohio	3/77	DR		—	1.28		(1) –3–4
Oregon	2/76	DR		—	1.38		(1) –4
Pennsylvania	10/75	1,187,296	2.96	4	1.23		1 –2–3–4
Puerto Rico	4/75	88,700	2.89	5		2.69	(1)–2 –4
Rhode Island	2/75	102,074	3.60	2		1.76	(1) –3–4
Vermont	2/74	46,376	3.78	1		1.90	(1)–2 –4
Washington	4/73	DR		—		2.45	(1) –4
Total		5,077,980					

NOTES: DR = debt repaid. Ohio never actually drew on its established credit.

[a] Wages in calendar year 1977.

[b] Reserve multiple: reserve ratio (reserve as percentage of total wages) times highest benefit-cost ratio (benefits as percentage of total wages) in previous twelve-month period. Reserve multiples less than the 1.5 norm are listed in the left-hand column, those greater than 1.5 in the right-hand column.

[c] 1 = No waiting period or, in parentheses, waiting period compensable after specified period of unemployment.
2 = Uniform duration.
3 = Dependents' benefits or variable maximum.
4 = Flexible maximum, rising automatically with wages.

SOURCE: U.S. Department of Labor.

21

TABLE 3

Taxable Wages as a Proportion of Total Wages Nationally, 1957–1978

Year	Proportion	Year	Proportion
1957	0.650	1968	0.517
1958	0.636	1969	0.497
1959	0.617	1970	0.477
1960	0.611	1971	0.452
1961	0.600	1972	0.517
1962	0.590	1973	0.497
1963	0.581	1974	0.476
1964	0.570	1975	0.452
1965	0.558	1976	0.465
1966	0.553	1977	0.451
1967	0.533	1978	0.496

SOURCE: U.S. Department of Labor.

little attention. Some states became accustomed, one might almost say addicted, to the low range of tax rates made possible by the previous history of excessive reserves. Second, persistent inflation played a significant role, especially in connection with the taxable wage base. As wages rose, benefits in many states automatically rose with them, but taxes did not do the same because the taxable base remained fixed. Hence a gap tended to develop between fund outflow and inflow. Taxable wages are shown in table 3 as a proportion of total wages nationally for the years covered by this review. Every year, without interruption, the proportion fell until 1972, when Congress raised the tax base to $4,200 (from $3,000) and again until 1976 and 1978, when Congress raised the base to $6,000. It is a decade since taxable wages were regularly as much as half of total wages. The decline in the tax base could have been offset by repeated increases in the tax rate, but whereas the change in the tax base was automatic, a change in the tax rate would have required legislative initiative, which was not always forthcoming.

Another aspect of the same phenomenon was the tendency of some states to think in terms of absolute dollar amounts when considering the adequacy of their reserves. Given the growth in the covered labor force, and inflation, the same number of dollars in a reserve fund represented a diminishing amount of protection. As late as 1978 the administrator of the Illinois Bureau of Employment Security told Congress that Illinois was "by any objective standard

TABLE 4

Numbers of States with Waiting Periods, 1945–1978

Year	Waiting Period		
	Two weeks	One week	Zero weeks
1945	13	37	1
1955	0	47	4
1965	0	48	3
1975	0	32	19
1978	0	30	21

Source: U.S. Department of Labor.

reasonably well prepared for the recession" because in 1974 Illinois "had a positive balance in the trust fund of $505 million, more than twice the amount of benefits the State had ever paid in a single year." [4] The more relevant fact was that the 1974 reserve amounted to only 1.4 percent of total wages. Since Illinois had in 1958 experienced a benefit-cost rate of 1.7 of total wages, its 1974 reserve was clearly inadequate by the norm of the reserve multiple.

Third, benefit provisions were being liberalized during the period when reserves were declining. For example, benefit duration expanded at both ends. Many states shortened or entirely eliminated the waiting period. Between 1945 (when reserves were at their peak) and 1978 the states changed the lengths of waiting periods as shown in table 4.[5]

Duration also lengthened at the other end. The number of weeks available to claimants grew both in the regular program and in triggered extensions of it. In the regular program, average potential duration grew from 19.8 weeks in 1946 to 24.3 weeks in 1975. ("Potential duration" is a measure of the number of weeks of benefits available to actual claimants.) Then, in 1970, the regular program was permanently enlarged to include a special extension of benefit duration whenever unemployment reached specified levels. These extended benefits are included in the benefit-cost rates shown in the tables. In the 1974–1975 recession, the states' share of extended benefits raised cost rates about a quarter of 1 percent on the average.

[4] U.S. Congress, House, Subcommittee on Public Assistance and Unemployment Compensation of the Committee on Ways and Means, Hearings on H.R. 8291, August 10 and 11, 1978, p. 256.

[5] Some of the states in the "zero weeks" column paid for the waiting period retroactively after a specified period of unemployment.

The benefit amount tended to rise faster in the later period than in the earlier periods of the program not only because of inflation but also because more states had adopted the "flexible maximum," that is, a provision that automatically raises the maximum benefit amount as total wages rise. As of 1978, thirty-six states had this automatic escalator device, whereas in 1945, when reserves were at their peak, none had it. Also, some states used an absolute amount of wages as an eligibility requirement. Under the impact of inflation, such a requirement became unrealistically low and admitted more claimants than had been planned for. All these changes on the benefit side of the program represented increased costs of which the states were not sufficiently aware in their planning.

One commonly offered explanation of the states' fiscal collapse finds little support in the data. It is commonly asserted that the unemployment insurance system had to sustain a steep secular rise in unemployment. If true, this development by itself would go far to absolve the states from blame—because the single most significant cause of rising unemployment insurance costs is rising unemployment and because large changes in the amount of unemployment can rarely be foreseen. The statistics do not bear out the basic assertion, however.

It is true that since 1950 there has been a secular rise in the general unemployment rate. As shown below, in data from the *Monthly Report on the Labor Force*, the average unemployment rate in the later period of prosperity did not sink as low as in the previous period of prosperity, whereas in the later recession period the average rate was higher than in the previous period of recession.

Prosperity: 1950–1956: 4.1 percent   1963–1969: 4.3 percent
Recession: 1957–1962: 5.7 percent   1970–1976: 6.2 percent

The difference is particularly marked when single years are compared. The highest unemployment rate previously was 6.8 percent in 1958. In 1975, however, the rate reached 9.3 percent, and in 1976 it was still 8.6 percent.

This rise in the general unemployment rate is not reflected, however, in the insured unemployment rate, the chief determinant of cost rates.[6] Averages of insured unemployment (taken from table

---

[6] One reason for the rising trend in general unemployment is the growing proportion of new entrants, especially youth and women, in the labor force. Because new entrants are not eligible for unemployment benefits, it is understandable that the insured unemployment rate may not follow closely the general unemployment rate. For the most recent development of the proposition that the amount of unemployment is the main determinant of benefit costs, see Saul J. Blaustein

21) for the corresponding periods show that the trend of the insured unemployment rate has been down rather than up.

Prosperity: 1951–1956: 3.3 percent   1964–1969: 2.6 percent
Recession: 1957–1963: 4.7 percent   1970–1976: 3.8 percent

Where the national average was 3.3 percent in the earlier prosperous period (1951–1956), it was only 2.6 percent in the next prosperous period (1964–1969). Where the average rate for the earlier recessionary period (1957–1963) was 4.7 percent, it was only 3.8 percent for the next period of recession (1970–1976). This trend is manifest not only in the totals for the United States but even for the eight states that had the largest debts and would be most likely to show a sharp rise in insured unemployment. In all but three of these states (Vermont, Connecticut, and Delaware) the later periods of prosperity and recession show lower rates than the respective earlier periods. Even for these three, the increases are too slight to offer a significant explanation for these states' financial collapse.

The claimants drawing extended benefits are not included in the insured unemployment rates given in table 21, but for two reasons their omission is not important for the present analysis. First, extended benefits do not add greatly to the overall costs. Even in 1975, as mentioned above, the states' share of extended benefits added only about a quarter of 1 percent to the average benefit-cost rate. Second, extended benefits represent not so much an independent rise in the unemployment rate as a liberalization of benefit provisions, specifically of the duration provision. Hence extended benefits may not be regarded as a factor independent of the liberalization of benefits in explaining the states' failure to anticipate costs.

To predict the course of unemployment is difficult and will probably always remain so. To translate any assumed amount of unemployment into a benefit-cost rate is an additional, an actuarial, difficulty. It was this double difficulty that caused most private insurance companies of the 1920s to doubt that insurance against unemployment could be provided. The years of experience under compulsory unemployment compensation have, however, contributed greatly to actuarial science as applied to unemployment. Especially in the 1950s, under the leadership of the federal actuaries Woytinsky and Wermel, the states learned to make usable long-term projections of benefit-cost ratios and the resulting required taxes.

and Paul J. Kozlowski, *Interstate Differences in Unemployment Insurance Benefit Costs: A Cross Section Study* (Kalamazoo, Mich.: W. E. Upjohn Institute for Employment Research, 1978).

The financial expertise developed during this period lapsed somewhat in later years at both the federal and state levels as problems seemed solved and trained personnel were lost and were not replaced. To some extent the recent collapse of state funds is traceable to inadequate actuarial analysis. In an excellent background paper prepared for the NCUC, Russell L. Hibbard analyzed the relationship between solvency and such practices as the noncharging of benefits.[7] Whether the states failed to perceive the actuarial relationship or whether the political factor mentioned below was operative, the result was the same—funds declined.

To some extent, the cause must be sought in limitations of the political process. Even when state administrators made the needs of the program known to state legislators, the latter sometimes neglected to take the recommended steps. There was at work the common political temptation to try to please all parties by increasing benefits and lowering taxes simultaneously. At work also was the more substantive political consideration that ample reserve funds tended to invite "raids" in the form of demands for more liberal benefits. This consideration has always been and probably always will be a major political obstacle to the maintenance of adequate reserves. Legislators were also influenced by the consideration that a reserve fund immobilized dollars that might better be put to work in the state's economy.[8]

The general impression left by a review of the 1970s is that of an exceptional experience. First, extraordinarily high reserves accumulated during the extraordinary event of the war, thereafter beguiling states into a euphoric disregard of financial realities. Contributing in a similar way was the extraordinarily long period of prosperity, the longest on record, during the 1960s. It was this prosperity that allowed a continual liberalization of the program to take place without adequate recognition of its long-term financial impact. An unusually rapid and persistent inflation contributed in several ways to the gradual attrition of the real value of the reserves. Congress repeatedly extended the duration of benefits without allowing time for the accumulation of the necessary reserves. Although only the state's share of extended benefits contributed

[7] Russell L. Hibbard, "Solvency Measures and Experience Rating," in National Commission on Unemployment Compensation, *Unemployment Compensation: Studies and Research*, vol. 2 (Washington, D.C., July 1980), pp. 329-38.

[8] Some states, like Michigan and Delaware, deliberately followed a policy of keeping reserves low but structuring a tax schedule that would respond quickly to a heavy benefit drain. In this policy the legislators were supported by, and probably influenced by, the dominant firms in their states.

directly to the state's debts, all benefits were to be financed eventually by a tax on the same employers, whether levied by state or federal governments, and thus contributed to the general financial stringency. Then came the very heavy unemployment of the 1970s, laying an unusually heavy burden on an unusually weakened system. The experience of the 1970s must be interpreted in the light of the exceptional nature of the period.

Individual State Experience

Behind the national averages lie the very dissimilar experiences of the individual states. Since the states do not have a common pocketbook but are each responsible for their own costs, ideally the experience of each state should be studied separately. This is impossible at present, however, and a useful alternative is to examine two groups of states whose experience is especially significant. The one group consists of the states with the largest debts; the other comprises the handful of large states that account for over half of all covered workers.

States Deepest in Debt. Before the 1975 recession, only three states had been forced to borrow: Alaska, Michigan, and Pennsylvania. All had repaid their debts; Michigan, indeed, had never actually used its loan. In the recent recession, however, twenty-two states—along with the District of Columbia, Puerto Rico, and the Virgin Islands, making twenty-five jurisdictions in all—became insolvent and had to borrow (table 19). Repayment was made promptly by seven states—Florida, Hawaii, Maryland, Nevada, Ohio,[9] Oregon, and Washington—leaving fifteen states (eighteen jurisdictions) still in debt at the start of 1979.

Of these fifteen states, only eight had a debt that equaled 1.5 percent or more of the states' total wages (table 2, column 3): Vermont, Rhode Island, Connecticut, Pennsylvania, New Jersey, Illinois, Delaware, and Michigan.[10] These represent the chief instances of failure to remain financially solvent. In their experience, if anything, grounds might be found for concluding that the states had failed and that financial responsibility, in whole or in part, should be placed elsewhere, presumably with the federal government.

[9] See footnote 3.

[10] These percentages are in terms of 1977 wages, the latest available at the time the table was constructed. The percentages would be smaller expressed in terms of current wages. For example, by the end of 1980, the debt of Pennsylvania was down to 2.3 percent of 1979 wages and that of Illinois was down to 1.4 percent. Inflation and other factors will continue to shrink these percentages automatically.

The financial experience of the eight states during the period 1957–1976 is presented in two tables and analyzed in a third. Table 17 summarizes their experience by averages for three subperiods: 1957–1962, a time of high unemployment that included two recessions; 1963–1969, a time of unprecedented prolonged prosperity; and 1970–1976, another period of high unemployment that included two recessions. Table 18 shows for each of the eight states the year-by-year experience underlying the averages.

This experience is analyzed in table 5. In judging the performance of these states, two general criteria are available: the cost burden they had to bear and the tax effort they made in response. The seven columns of the table present various aspects of these two criteria. In general, the states with the most check marks are the best performers and hence are least open to criticism for incurring debt. Contrariwise, the states with the fewest checks show the worst performance and are most open to the charge of poor financial management.

The first column looks to the size of the state's reserve fund at the end of 1969. For all these states, the period 1963–1969 was one of unprecedented prosperity. At the end of such a period, if ever, their reserve funds should have been adequate. The measure of adequacy used in the table is the admittedly rough but generally accepted norm of a "reserve multiple" of 1.5, recommended as a *minimum* safety measure by the states themselves in 1959, as I noted above. Only two states (Vermont and Rhode Island) met this minimum criterion. These two could plead that at least according to the conventional wisdom of the time, they had been provident. The other states could not claim even this much.

The second column considers whether the state's benefit-cost rate in the 1970s was notably higher than in any previous period. To the extent that it was, the state had at least the excuse that nothing in its experience had prepared it for the unprecedented benefit drain of the later period. Five of the eight states could make this claim. Pennsylvania, Illinois, and Michigan could not; they had earlier encountered even higher benefit costs. Indeed, Pennsylvania and Michigan had been forced to borrow previously. On the basis of past experience, both states clearly should have used the 1960s to build their reserves to at least the minimum reserve multiple.

Columns 3 and 4 ask whether these states, which had a worse-than-average record of debt, could offer as one excuse that they also had a worse-than-average benefit-cost rate, either in the 1960s or in the 1970s. Only three of the eight (Vermont, Rhode Island, and New Jersey) could offer this excuse in the 1960s. All the rest had a

TABLE 5

EVALUATION OF FINANCIAL PERFORMANCE OF EIGHT STATES WITH LARGEST DEBTS, BY SELECTED CRITERIA

State	Reserve Multiple 1.5 or Better at End of 1969 (1)	Benefit-Cost Rate Notably Higher in 1970s Than in Earlier Recessions (2)	Benefit-Cost Rate Notably Higher Than National Average		Tax Rate Notably Higher Than National Average		Tax Base Higher Than Federal Requirement (7)
			In 1960s (3)	In 1970s (4)	In 1960s (5)	In 1970s (6)	
Vermont	+	+	+	+	+	+	+
Rhode Island	+	+	+	+	+	+	+
Connecticut		+		+		+	+
Pennsylvania					+	+	+
New Jersey		+	+	+	+		
Illinois				+			
Delaware		+			+	+	+
Michigan							+

SOURCES: Column 1, table 2; columns 2–7, table 18.

29

lighter-than-average burden during that period, when reserves could have been strengthened most easily. A comparison of column 3 with column 1 reveals that of the six states with inadequate reserves, only one (New Jersey) could offer as an excuse that its unemployment costs during the 1960s were higher than in the average state.

Column 4 asks the same question as column 3 but with regard to the 1970s. Here six of the eight states can offer the excuse of having had a heavier-than-average benefit burden. Illinois and Delaware, however, had a lighter burden than even the average state, and the average state did not have to borrow.

Column 5 looks at the other side of the financial operation, the inflow of funds. It asks whether the tax rate imposed by these states in the prosperous period of the 1960s was notably higher than that of the average state. To the extent that it was, there is the basis for a claim to financial responsibility. Five of the eight could make this claim. Connecticut, Illinois, and Delaware, however, taxed their employers at rates about average, or even below average, during the opportune period of the 1960s.

Column 6 asks the same question with regard to the 1970s, and here the eight states show up somewhat better: Six of the eight—all except Illinois and Delaware (again)—did tax their employers at a rate notably higher than that of the average state.

Enlarging the taxable base is another way of increasing the tax flow, and column 7 asks whether any of the eight states took this obvious step. Their record is quite good in this respect. All except one (Illinois) at some time raised their tax base to a level higher than that required by federal law, reflecting the state's own initiative.

On the basis of these criteria, Vermont and Rhode Island, followed by New Jersey, are the least open to criticism. Although their debts are relatively largest, they also have the best record of responsible financial management—or at least the most plausible excuses for their bankruptcy. At the other end of the spectrum, Illinois has the worst record, closely followed by Delaware. Illinois does not rate a single check; Delaware rates only two. Although neither of these states faced above-average benefit-cost rates, they seemed unable to find enough money to fund their below-average costs.

A final characteristic of the eight states is supplied by column 6 of table 2, which shows selected benefit provisions of the debtor states. As may be seen, all eight states had at least two of the more liberal provisions. Vermont and Rhode Island had three, whereas Connecticut, Pennsylvania, and Illinois had all four. Not much can be concluded from this characteristic. Still, it does serve to indicate that the eight are not poor, hard-pressed states with high costs that forced them to accept a minimal program. They seem rather to have been states that felt the need to strengthen their programs but neglected to calculate the taxes needed to support their more costly programs.

Could these states have done better? It is certain that they could. Considering the high reserves inherited from the war years, considering also the long prosperous period of the 1960s, when even the New England states had low benefit-cost rates, considering finally—and most significantly—the relatively small size of the unemployment insurance tax, it seems clear that any and all of these states could have accumulated enough reserves in the 1960s to have seen them through the unemployment of the 1970s. Certainly no persuasive evidence to the contrary has thus far been presented, and the burden of proof rests on the proposition that the states are unable to meet their own costs.

The Ten Largest States. Covered employment is distributed very unequally among the fifty-one jurisdictions, with about half of it (55 percent) concentrated in ten states. Special interest therefore attaches to the experience of these large states. The ten are listed in table 6 in descending order of debt ratio at the end of 1978. The table also shows their average benefit-cost rate for the period 1970–1976, their reserve multiple at the end of 1969, and their percentage of total covered employment.

Inevitably there is some overlap between the ten largest states and the eight states with the largest debts, but not so much as might be expected. Only four (Pennsylvania, New Jersey, Illinois, and Michigan) of the large states appear among the states with the largest debts (table 5); the other six large states either escaped borrowing altogether or borrowed less than some smaller states.

Eight of the ten large states (all except California and Texas) had been forced to borrow.[11] Of the eight borrowers, only three (Massachusetts, New York, and Florida) could offer the defense that they had begun the 1970s with a reserve multiple that met at least the minimum solvency standard of 1.5. Five (Pennsylvania, New Jersey, Michigan, Massachusetts, and New York) could offer the defense that they had experienced a benefit-cost rate during the 1970s that was higher than the national average of 1.28. Illinois was unable to offer either defense.

The four states showing no debt at the end of 1978 account for over 25 percent of the covered workers. Of the four, Florida and

[11] As I explained in footnote 3, Ohio never actually used its loan.

TABLE 6

Profile of the Ten Largest States at the End of 1978

State	Debt Ratio[a] (1)	Average Benefit-Cost Rate, 1970–76[b] (2)	Reserve Multiple, 1969[c] (3)	Percentage of Covered Employment (4)
Pennsylvania	2.96	1.61	1.23	5.5
New Jersey	2.61	2.12	1.22	3.3
Illinois	2.09	1.03	1.17	5.4
Michigan	1.70	1.63	0.85	4.5
Massachusetts	1.38	2.03	1.74	2.8
New York	0.52	1.54	1.91	8.1
California	0	1.59	1.43	10.8
Florida	0	0.93	2.42	3.8
Ohio	0	0.92	1.28	5.5
Texas	0	0.36	2.19	5.8

a Debt at end of 1978 as percentage of 1977 total payrolls.
b Benefits as percentage of total payrolls.
c Reserve ratio divided by highest twelve-month benefit-cost ratio.
Sources: Columns 1 and 3, table 2; column 2, table 17; column 4, U.S. Department of Labor, Unemployment Insurance Service.

Ohio had repaid their borrowings, whereas California and Texas never had to borrow. The favorable record of Florida, Ohio, and Texas is easily understood: Their costs were less than those of the other large states. The success of California in avoiding borrowing despite a cost rate higher than the national average of 1.28 holds the promise of a moral and calls for closer examination.

The history of California's reserve fund generally resembles that of the nation. In 1957 the state's reserve amounted to 5.73 percent of total wages but was allowed to decline year after year, until by 1965 it was only 2.28 percent. In the four prosperous years of 1966–1969, California's reserve increased somewhat, but only to 3.23 percent, a reserve multiple of 1.43. During the ensuing period, 1970–1976, the reserve ratio dropped every year. The descent was halted just short of bankruptcy by very vigorous tax efforts in 1975.

Early in 1975, in a bulletin dated February 12, the California Taxpayers' Association (Cal-Tax) alerted its members to the possibility that the state unemployment insurance fund might encounter trouble that year. In a series of bulletins, the association explained to its members that although the fund then contained a billion dollars, it might have to be strengthened by tax increases in the coming year because of heavy payouts and the cash flow problems of 1976. The bulletins show a thorough grasp of the intricacies of unemployment insurance financing. Later in the year, when the legislature considered legislation to increase taxes substantially, the taxpayers were prepared to cooperate. The board of directors of the California Taxpayers' Association made the deliberate choice of "refinancing" rather than borrowing. One of the considerations influencing their decision was the argument that if the state borrowed, the federal tax would eventually be increased by law, automatically, and the money thus paid would go into federal coffers and would not be experience-rated. If the state tax increased instead, the added taxes would go into employers' state reserve accounts. The actuarial firm regularly hired by California to review its financing disagreed, recommending borrowing instead of refinancing. The gist of the firm's argument was summed up in its off-the-record observation: "Just offer any business-man an interest-free loan . . . " Perhaps because of his presidential aspirations, Governor Brown was nevertheless opposed to borrowing. A bankrupt California would not provide a helpful national image.

As a result of all these influences, the California legislature passed a bill toward the end of 1975 that raised both the tax base and the tax rates, increasing the tax flow by $600 million, a 66 percent increase in fund income. The same bill also raised the minimum and maximum benefits. This vigorous action was taken while the recession was still at its worst. California's experience certainly strengthens the case for state responsibility. It also buttresses the argument that the unemployment insurance tax is not of such a magnitude as to threaten a state's economy.

It may be noted in passing that California, almost more than any other state, has generally taken the responsibility of determining, and frequently manipulating, its own taxable wage base. California raised the tax base to $3,600 in 1960, to $3,800 in 1962, and to $4,100 in 1966. It lowered the base to $3,800 in 1967. With all the other states it raised the base to $4,200 in 1972 but then, on its own initiative, raised it to $7,000 in 1976. These repeated adjustments were largely the result of a "rocking wage base" provision adopted by the California legislature in 1965, a provision whose wisdom is questioned by many financial experts.

Illinois sharply contrasts with California. Both before and during the 1970s, Illinois experienced below-average cost rates (table 17). Yet it has been compelled to borrow every year since 1975 (table 19) and at the end of 1978 owed almost $1 billion. The explanation of Illinois's bankruptcy is to be found in the decisions made during two periods, in the 1960s and in 1975. Of the two, the former was by far the more important.

During the prosperous 1960s, Illinois failed to build its reserve fund to the size that experience had shown to be needed. The fault did not lie with the agency. Having analyzed the actuarial situation accurately, the agency repeatedly warned the decision makers (the governor, the legislature, and the advisory board) that the fund was inadequate and would become weaker unless taxes increased. This warning was offered at least every two years and sometimes annually. Nevertheless, the legislature did not act. To understand why, one must understand the function of the Illinois Advisory Board.

In Illinois, the legislative process has relied since 1939 on the bills agreed upon by the advisory board of nine people (three members each from labor, management, and the public) appointed by the governor.[12] In years when the board did not agree on a bill, the legislature declined to act. During the 1960s, the employer members of the advisory board refused to agree to the tax increases urged by the agency. The labor and public members of the advisory board tended to concentrate their attention on the benefit side of the program and to leave tax matters to the employer members. The result was a series of agreed-upon bills that made some modest improvement in benefits but saw no increase in taxes.

Why did the employer members reject the agency's warnings? Primarily because they feared that a larger reserve would invite "raids" on the fund. Since 1959, the Illinois law has specified that the fund must consist of at least $450 million. During the period 1965–1969, the fund grew to over $500 million. Employers feared that an even larger fund would look like a lot of money to people innocent of actuarial expertise. On one occasion, for example, the governor urged the employer members of the advisory board to agree to a benefit increase proposed by labor on the ground that "it will not cost anything; the money is in the fund, and we will not have to raise taxes."

In fact, however, the prescribed $450 million was inadequate during the 1960s and grew less adequate with each passing year—

[12] The advisory board is, of course, only advisory. Its agreed-upon bills had such influence only because the governor and the legislature found the arrangement effective and politically convenient. Illinois was one of a small handful of states that preferred to work through the agreed-upon bills of an advisory body. For the full story of the Illinois Advisory Board, see Joseph M. Becker, *Shared Government in Employment Security* (New York: Columbia University Press, 1959), pp. 143-72.

because of the real growth in the size of the Illinois economy (more firms doing more business with a larger labor force) and because of continuous inflation. When the agency accurately analyzed this situation and issued its annual warnings, the employer members of the advisory board returned a vague assurance that if the fund were ever threatened by insolvency, the legislature could be convened in an emergency session to raise the necessary taxes. The fund was therefore allowed to remain at an actuarially inadequate level.

In 1975, the story was rather different. The elections in the fall of 1972 had returned a Democratic governor and a Democratic majority in both houses. Labor judged that it could do better by ignoring the advisory board and going directly to the legislature. In 1975, a bill was introduced containing nearly all the long-term UI objectives of labor. To the surprise of everyone, even of its supporters, the bill moved through the legislature with few changes. It was probably helped by the rising tide of unemployment. When employers saw that its enactment was likely, they proposed to labor that it be amended to include a tax increase sufficient to support the increased benefits. Labor refused. They feared that the inclusion of a tax provision would jeopardize the entire bill. In all probability, the same thought had occurred to the employer representatives who suggested the tax increase. The lobbyists on both sides were well aware that people who have to be elected, whether to state or federal office, much prefer voting for benefits to voting for taxes. The governor's predecessor, Ogilvie, had been defeated partly because he had supported the enactment of a state income tax, and his successor, Walker, had run on a platform of no tax increases. Thus in the same year that California was deciding to increase taxes and benefits, Illinois was deciding to increase only benefits.

The Illinois experience provides two important lessons. First, it illustrates the single greatest obstacle to rational financing of unemployment insurance: the failure of legislators to understand the meaning of a *reserve*. They tend to think of the hundreds of millions of dollars in the fund as "unused" and available for increased benefits without an increase in taxes, in other words, available for a "raid." It is only this tendency on the part of the legislators that supplies any justification for the refusal of Illinois employers to support tax increases in the prosperous 1960s. Second, Illinois employers profited greatly by following the path that they did. That profit came from two sources. They had the use of almost a billion dollars for half a dozen years without cost (the federal loans were interest free). Also, they will be paying back the loan in inflation-depreciated dollars. The availability of such a handsome profit is another obstacle to rational financing. In this case, however, the solution is simple: The federal loans need only carry sufficient interest charges. Of the remaining fifty states, many more resemble California than resemble Illinois. Indeed, most of the states have an even better record than California, and no other state has as bad a record as Illinois.

Conclusions

Past. The more the experience of the 1970s is analyzed, the less it seems to be an example of long-term decline caused by basic weaknesses in the system and the more it resembles a short-term difficulty from which the system has the innate health to recover. The exceptionally large number of states needing to borrow may be explained by exceptional circumstances. The lessons learned from the experience will make its repetition in the future less likely. There is at work in the system now both a more sophisticated financial expertise and a more responsible political awareness.

The post-mortems conducted by the states have revealed with great clarity the causes of their bankruptcy or near bankruptcy. These analyses are proving useful to the administrators of the program in their dealings with state legislatures and tax-paying employers, the more because a strengthened federal actuarial unit is now in a position to offer improved technical assistance to the states. Finally, the states are gradually including in their laws provisions that automatically guard state reserves. An increasing number of states are making use, for example, of the "common account," which automatically provides for the financing of noncharged and ineffectively charged benefits.[13] They are also making use of a tax base that automatically rises with total covered wages. History shows that provisions that perform a clearly useful function, after being introduced by a few leaders, tend to spread to the rest of the states. On the whole, solvency is likely to be better protected in the future than in the past, partly because of the recent jolting experience.

The only development that could cancel out the salutary effects of the experience would be the remission of the debts. Proposals for remission have won little support, and outright remission seems very unlikely. The nation seems too committed—still—to market principles to be comfortable requiring the employers of a state like California to pay the debts of the employers of a state like Illinois.

[13] For an explanation of how the common account operates, see index under "Common account" in Joseph M. Becker, *Experience Rating in Unemployment Insurance* (Baltimore: Johns Hopkins University Press, 1972).

Bills have been introduced in Congress—specifically, by Brodhead and Javits—that would have some of the effect of debt remission. Since these refer not to solvency but to the distribution of the tax burden, they are treated in chapter 3, on cost equalization.

If the federal government, rather than the state governments, had been responsible for the solvency of the system, would solvency have been better maintained? Although the question thus phrased is too ambiguous to be answered clearly (does the question assume federal control from the beginning? federal control over benefits and other provisions? sole reliance on an employer tax? reliance on an experience-rated tax, making each state still responsible, in effect, for its own costs? and so on), the following observations are at least relevant to the answer.

If pooled nationally, the same total reserve funds would have provided more protection against insolvency. Whether the same total reserve would have accumulated is questionable. Congress would have been under much the same political pressures as the states to keep taxes at the lowest possible level consistent with the vague notion of a "safe" reserve. Congress would have been more open to the possible use of deficit financing and would hence have been under less pressure to accumulate reserves against an unforeseen benefit drain. The record of Congress in the financing of OASDHI reveals a much greater willingness to depart from "insurance" financing than any state has manifested. The record of Congress in financing the programs of extended benefits and of federal supplemental benefits shows the same tendency to pay benefits now and raise the necessary taxes later. The National Commission on Unemployment Compensation noted "the magnitude of the benefit costs resulting from the various federally enacted extensions during this period before sufficient reserves had been accumulated to pay them." [14] If the federal government had been responsible for solvency and had in fact followed the policy of keeping reserves as low as possible, the final result would probably not have been substantially different. During the unexpectedly high unemployment of the 1970s, the UI fund would have borrowed from general revenues, and the amount borrowed might very well have been greater.

A second question is more realistic. If a federal solvency standard had been in operation, would the states have had a better record in maintaining solvency? This question is more realistic both because it is more measurable and because such a standard is currently under

[14] *Unemployment Compensation: Final Report* (Washington, D.C.: National Commission on Unemployment Compensation, July 1980), p. 78.

serious consideration. On the assumption that the standard would have been the reserve multiple recommended by the states, then if the minimum of the recommended range, a multiple of 1.5, had been the standard, the debts of the states would be less today by at least one-quarter. A standard using a higher multiple would, of course, have had a greater effect. A standard at the upper end of the range, namely 3.0, would have resulted in reserves easily capable of weathering the recent recession. It would also have resulted in excess reserves in most states.

Present. If we assume that their debts will not be remitted, how serious is the condition of the debtors? At the end of 1978, only seven states (Vermont, Rhode Island, Connecticut, Pennsylvania, New Jersey, Illinois, and Delaware) were faced with debts greater than 2 percent of total wages (table 2). Six of the seven states were in the Northeast—so that the problem was to some extent regional rather than general—and four of them were small.

The percentages of table 2 are in terms of 1977 covered wages. If they were expressed in terms of current wages, all these percentages would be smaller. The continuous growth of the labor force and of inflation generates a constantly growing amount of total wages. Fixed dollar amounts of debts expressed as a percentage of constantly growing total wages represent a constantly shrinking debt burden. Inflation especially represents a costless shrinking of the burden of the debtor, the more so when the debt is interest free. By the time the drafts come due, the percentages of table 2 will be significantly smaller. Already by the end of 1980 the number of states with debts greater than 2 percent of total wages had been reduced from seven to four (Vermont, Rhode Island, Connecticut, and Pennsylvania)—the combined result of some repayments and the growth factor just described.[15]

Some of the states with the largest debts may need an extension of time within which to make repayment. The debtors have already received such a grace period, which could be further extended if the economy should turn down before repayment is completed. If the economy worsens greatly over a protracted period for the debtor states, the situation will require remedies other than unemployment insurance. When Lord William Beveridge came to write his master

[15] As of December 31, 1980, ten states had repaid their debts in full: Washington, Massachusetts, Alabama, Hawaii, Nevada, Oregon, Missouri, Florida, Montana, and New York. Additional loans had been made to other states, however; so the total debt outstanding was about the same as that shown in table 2. (Michigan paid off its total loan in December 1979 but borrowed again immediately in January 1980.)

plan for Britain's system of social programs, he laid down two basic conditions necessary for any rational social insurance system. One was a reasonably high level of employment over the long run. If that condition obtains, the states can meet their financial responsibilities. Otherwise social insurance, as distinct from social assistance, is not usable.

Future. One way of guarding against insolvency is to accumulate reserves large enough to meet any conceivable emergency. Still, because such large reserves immobilize an undesirably large proportion of available economic funds, it is more practicable to combine a smaller reserve with a loan fund or a reinsurance fund or both. The principal difference between the two is that a loan fund requires repayment, whereas a reinsurance fund makes nonrepayable grants. Although there is substantial agreement that the "smaller reserve" should be large enough to make recourse to either of the emergency funds rare, there is little agreement about whether the reserve should be governed by a federal standard. These three matters (the loan fund, the reinsurance fund, and the federal standard) are bound to figure in any future discussion of the solvency problem.

Loan fund. The unemployment insurance system has made provisions for loans since 1945, and any future system will undoubtedly include some kind of loan fund. Even if a reinsurance fund is set up, provision must be made against the contingency that some state some time may find the reinsurance grant either not available to it or inadequate to enable the state to continue paying benefits. A loan fund is the ultimate life net.

Any future loan fund should charge interest on its loans, either at the rate being earned by the system's trust fund held by the U.S. Treasury or at the rate paid currently by the Treasury on its own borrowings. Interest-free loans constitute a strong inducement for a state to keep its trust fund lower than is actuarially sound. As the actuarial firm said to the California agency, "What businessman would refuse an interest-free loan?" It becomes logical to borrow. This logic holds even apart from inflation. Since inflation means that a loan will be repaid in cheaper dollars, however, it adds to the inducement to borrow and repay rather than to prepay. Furthermore, the loans are financed from taxes levied on the employers of all the states. If the loans are interest free, they constitute a subsidy paid to some states by other states and thus introduce into the program an additional element of cost equalization. In chapter 3 I discuss the extent to which cost equalization may or may not be desirable.

Reinsurance fund. Reinsurance is a form of insurance against catastrophe. Each member of a group of insurers contributes to a central fund to support any member who has an extraordinarily unfavorable experience. Reinsurance relieves all the insurers of the necessity of accumulating excessively large reserves to meet the occasional catastrophic event.

It differs fundamentally from cost equalization (see chapter 3), with which it is often confused, sometimes intentionally. The two differ in their objectives. Where cost equalization seeks to protect against inequality, reinsurance seeks to protect against uncertainty. In the case of pure reinsurance, it is not possible to predict which states are likely to receive a grant. (In cost equalization it is possible.) Reinsurance thus fulfills an essential condition of any genuine insurance, namely, that the actual occurrence insured against be uncertain.

Proposals to add a reinsurance fund have been made frequently over the life of the system. A genuine reinsurance plan was put forward in 1953 by Milton O. Loysen, administrator of the New York employment security agency, who had, appropriately, experience in the field of insurance. A decade later, in 1963, the Benefit Financing Committee of the Interstate Conference of Employment Security Agencies (ICESA) produced a refined version of the Loysen plan. Under the ICESA proposal, called catastrophe reinsurance, a fund would be established by a tax levied on all states. A state would become eligible for a grant when its benefit-cost rate exceeded 1.6 times its own average rate over the preceding five years. The grant would cover 60 percent of this excess cost. If the tax supporting such a plan were experience rated, so that states which drew on the fund more frequently would pay a somewhat higher tax, the plan would be pure reinsurance.

In recent years, ICESA shifted from this genuine and relatively simple reinsurance plan to a complex proposal that included substantial elements of cost equalization, especially financing from general revenues. William M. Brodhead submitted this proposal to Congress in 1979 in the form of H.R. 8292.[16] From time to time, ICESA has modified its plan and probably will continue to introduce changes.[17]

Plans have come from other sources also. In 1979, the states of Louisiana, Ohio, and Washington proposed their own reinsurance plans differing in various ways from the ICESA plan. Other groups also proposed alternatives to the ICESA plan. The California Tax-

[16] For a legislative analysis of H.R. 8292, see *Unemployment Insurance: Reinsurance and Cost Equalization Proposals*, American Enterprise Institute Legislative Analysis, no. 30 (Washington, D.C., 1978).

[17] In early 1980, the latest ICESA proposal was embodied in the Brodhead bill, H.R. 3937.

payers' Association submitted a genuine reinsurance plan of modest proportions to be financed by a uniform federal tax of 0.2 percent on all covered employers. Another group of employers submitted a plan of genuine reinsurance that was linked with an automatically adjusted tax base and was financed by a state tax that was experience rated.

The staff of the National Commission on Unemployment Compensation has put together a lengthy paper on reinsurance entitled "Issues and Options" that illustrates the wide variety of plans already proposed and suggests the almost endless combinations and modifications that may yet emerge. Here our concern is not with the details of concrete plans but rather with a few guiding principles useful for the evaluation of any plan:

1. In a genuine reinsurance plan, the pattern of grants to the states must be unpredictable. Reinsurance is thus not suitable protection against either seasonal or chronic unemployment. The question whether it is suitable as protection against cyclical unemployment must be answered with a distinction drawn from the following principle.

2. Reinsurance is intended as protection against catastrophic loss. The more nearly the plan insures against ordinary loss, the less it constitutes genuine reinsurance. As to cyclical unemployment, every state's trust fund should be able to withstand recessions of average severity, for these are a normal part of economic life. Given the success of practically all the trust funds in weathering the 1958 recession, the definition of catastrophic risk might include only events of greater severity.

3. The catastrophic risk should be defined in relation to each state's individual experience. Any attempt to define the risk in terms of some absolute norm common to all the states inevitably introduces an element of cost equalization. This is because the states differ predictably in their average rates of unemployment and in their benefit provisions.

4. The reinsurance fund must be financed by the participants. Whatever else it may be, a plan financed from general revenues is not reinsurance.

5. Payments made to the reinsurance fund by the participants should be experience rated. No matter how carefully the plan is constructed, it may result in systematic payments to a small number of states. There need be less concern about such an effect if the contributions to the plan are experience rated. The degrees of experience rating need not be 100 percent. As in the regular program, experience rating of less than 100 percent may still achieve the essential intended effects.

A reinsurance plan embodying the principles above would undoubtedly strengthen the unemployment insurance program. There are only two serious objections to such a plan. First, the definition of "catastrophe" may not remain constant. The normal political process that seems to affect all transfer payments may bring about a gradual relaxation of the conditions for receiving a grant. As that happens, any reinsurance plan is gradually affected by cost equalization. A larger and larger proportion of benefits is paid, not out of each state's trust fund, but out of a common reinsurance fund. If payments to the reinsurance fund are not experience rated, or if the degree of experience rating is also relaxed, the move toward cost equalization is accentuated. Second, any central fund would be under the direction of the federal government to a greater extent than are expenditures from each state's trust fund. This additional federal fund tends to increase federal influence, most likely through the imposition of additional federal standards.

Although reinsurance is a sensible and efficient device, it is not an essential one. A loan program also enables the states to limit the size of their reserves, and the system has had many years of successful experience with a loan program. The principal difference between loans and reinsurance is that loans must eventually be repaid. Thus the basic reason for preferring reinsurance to loans must be that the borrowing states are "unable" to make repayment. This reason leads directly to the issue of cost equalization and is treated in chapter 3.

Federal solvency standard. Such a standard, probably of the reserve-multiple type, would almost certainly strengthen the system's defenses against insolvency. True, some states that have usually kept reserves above the minimum standard might experience local political pressure to reduce their reserves to the minimum. In all probability, however, this effect would be more than offset by the action of the other states, which would have to increase taxes to meet the standard.

The operation of a standard would greatly ease the task of the state administrators and legislators. When taking the unpopular step of raising taxes, they could always disclaim responsibility and put the blame on the far-off federal bureaucrats. Whether such a shift in responsibility is desirable or not is more open to dispute. Some states would welcome the shift; others would not. At its midyear meeting in March 1979, the Interstate Conference of Employment Security Agencies voted 40 to 5 against any federal benefit standard. Although a benefit standard is more controversial than a solvency standard, the size of the negative vote and the fact that it was a reversal of ICESA's 1975 position probably reflect a generally lessened confidence in federal regulation.

42

A strict federal requirement that states repay all loans has the same final effect as a solvency standard—all states eventually raise the funds required to pay the covenanted benefits. Although the two are thus similar in their effect on solvency, they may differ in their effect on benefits. A debt that has to be repaid may provide an argument for deferring an increase in benefits. On the contrary, a standard that results in the accumulation of funds before benefits are paid may provide the basis for a decision to increase benefits.

On the other side of the ledger, there are some possible disadvantages accompanying a federal solvency standard. Apart from difficulties of administration, which exist but are solvable, there is the difficulty of enacting the "right" standard. States differ in their economic structures, in provisions of their UI programs, and consequently in their financial needs. No one standard is best for all states at all times.

On the assumption that the standard selected is generally similar to the reserve multiple of 1.5, some states would find themselves overfunded—in their judgment. They would object to the required reserve for two reasons: because dollars otherwise available for creating jobs in the state were being "retired" to the trust fund in Washington and because the availability of excess funds would invite demands for increased benefits.

Probably the chief objection to a federal standard, in the minds of its opponents, concerns none of these measurable effects but a general aversion to "federalization," that is, general suspicion of a further transfer of responsibility from the states to the federal government. For example, the existence of a federal standard would strengthen efforts to subsidize states that became insolvent while complying with the standard. Opponents fear that the acceptance of one standard will not only diminish state responsibility in the immediate area affected but will invite the imposition of additional standards in other areas. If a state cannot be trusted in this matter, can it be trusted in other matters? A principle may be affected: The location of the burden of proof may shift.

Until the present, the burden of proof has rested on any proposal to transfer responsibility from a smaller to a larger unit of society. Opponents argue that a federal standard has not been proved necessary to ensure solvency. On the contrary, the lessons learned from the recent recession, the growing financial expertise of the states, the availability of provisions in the UI law that guard solvency automatically, the possible availability of a reinsurance fund, and the certain availability of a loan fund—all combine to outweigh evidence thus far advanced that a federal solvency standard is needed.

3

Cost Sharing

State of the Question

Throughout the life of the unemployment insurance program, each state has been required to meet its own unemployment insurance costs. This requirement has resulted in a very unequal distribution of the total cost burden, as may be seen in figure 2, which shows cumulative benefit-cost rates by state for the period 1940–1978.[1] The long-run cost rate of Rhode Island has been four times that of Texas.[2] About 51 percent of the covered work force is in the first twenty-five states of the distribution, and about 49 percent in the remaining twenty-six states—an indication that large and small states are about equally represented among the high-cost and low-cost states. Geographically, however, there is a marked concentration of high-cost states in the North: of the first twenty-five states, only five are in the South or Southwest.

These data refer only to the "regular" unemployment insurance program and to the state share of extended benefits. They exclude the extended benefits that have been financed by a federal tax (on all covered employers or on all taxpayers) and hence have involved cost sharing. The sharing of the costs of extended benefits is not currently an issue and is not under discussion here.[3] This chapter is concerned

[1] The benefit-cost rate is the ratio of benefits, including the state's share of extended benefits, to total covered wages. Although the tax rate need not be the same as the cost rate in any one year, over the long run the tax rate must at least equal the cost rate.

[2] Alaska's cost rate has been six times that of Texas, but everything about Alaska is exceptional.

[3] How the costs of extended benefits came to be shared is too long a story to be recounted fully here. Briefly, after a series of meetings in the late 1960s, a committee of the Interstate Conference of Employment Security Agencies developed a recommendation that the federal government stand ready to finance half the costs of benefits paid beyond twenty-six weeks—paid by any state, under any conditions, at any time. The objective of the recommendation was the gradual extension of the duration of benefits in the regular program by the use of the federal carrot but according to each state's own specifications. Once introduced into Congress (1970) this simple proposal was transformed into a complex, obligatory, recession-triggered program, whose federal coloration and use of a national trigger were justified by the argument that a recession was a "national" problem.

solely with the issue of cost sharing in the regular unemployment insurance program.

There have been many proposals to achieve a greater equality of cost through some form of federal subsidy. Although they have usually borne the title of reinsurance, the proposals were really cost equalization. As will be recalled from the previous chapter, the two forms of subsidy differ fundamentally. Where the reason for reinsurance is the unforeseen nature of the burden, the reason for cost equalization is the excessive size of the burden, even though foreseen. Both seek to provide help for states that have experienced unusually high costs, but they differ in the way they define "unusual." In reinsurance, the norm of usual is a state's own previous experience, whereas in cost equalization the norm is some absolute level that applies to all states at all times. The norm most frequently proposed has been a cost rate of 2 percent of total wages. Any state that had a cost rate greater than this would be reimbursed from a central fund for all or part of the excess cost.

Cost equalization was first discussed by the Committee on Economic Security in 1934, and thereafter plans for cost equalization surfaced repeatedly—for example, in 1944 (S. 1730), in 1950 (H.R. 8059), in 1952 (H.R. 6954), in 1959 (H.R. 3547), and in 1965 (H.R. 8282). The 1965 proposal was supported strongly by the Johnson administration and might have been approved by Congress if it had not included a federal benefit standard.

One recent proposal was developed by the Interstate Conference of Employment Security Agencies and was introduced in Congress by William Brodhead of Michigan in 1979 as H.R. 3937. It was primarily a reinsurance plan but had elements of cost equalization. Because of these elements, states that regularly have higher than average levels of unemployment (seasonal, cyclical, or chronic), such as Washington, Michigan, or Rhode Island, would be eligible for a subsidy more often than states with lower than average unemployment, such as Colorado, Texas, or Virginia. Still, there was less cost sharing than in later versions put forward by the ICESA.

There is an indefinite number of ways of providing for cost sharing. Moreover, any concrete proposal submitted to Congress is almost certain to undergo modification in the normal course of legislative compromise. Rather than consider any particular plan, therefore, it seems more useful to discuss general principles.

The first principle has to do with the allocation of the burden of proof. The discussion here assumes that it rests on the proposal to share costs, an assumption consonant with the basic characteristics of the unemployment insurance program and the American economy.

The decision to make each state responsible for its own costs was reached after intense public debate, and this original decision has been reaffirmed repeatedly after numerous challenges. The principle of individual state responsibility has possessed the field and must be dislodged by proof.

Until the present the unemployment insurance program has been viewed as an extension of the wage system: Only regular wage earners are covered by the system, and their benefits are individually determined by the amount of their work and wages. It is entirely compatible with this view of the system to make each economic agent (state and employer) individually responsible for meeting the cost of the program, a regular cost of doing business. The decision to make unemployment insurance an extension of the wage system rests on the still more fundamental decision to make the competitive market the principal mechanism for the distribution of the nation's resources. Underlying *that* choice is the near-basic choice of the desired relationship between the individual and the group, described in chapter 1.

Given this allocation of the burden of proof, evidence is needed that the present system of financing has undesirable effects that would be lessened with more cost sharing. The possible undesirable effects are of two sorts, intrinsic and extrinsic to unemployment insurance—that is, effects on the unemployment insurance program itself and effects on the economy. The effects on unemployment insurance are by far the more significant because the primary objective of unemployment insurance is to aid the individual unemployed person, not to affect the general economy.

Intrinsic Effects

The argument for cost sharing stands or falls principally on whether or not it would cause unemployment insurance better to perform its primary function of aiding the unemployed. The proponents of cost sharing assume that a "better" program is one whose provisions are more uniform and more liberal. Because little formal effort has been made to prove the validity of either assumption, there is little evidence, or even argument, to address.

By simply equating inequality with inequity, proponents conclude that uniformity is better. But the unequal is not necessarily inequitable; if it were, the whole wage structure would be inequitable. This observation is relevant because of the close connection between unemployment insurance and the wage system, which gives unemployment insurance benefits the nature of an earned right and justifies the difference in the benefits paid to individual claimants. Moreover, recipients of unemployment insurance, unlike those receiving welfare and old-age insurance payments, are still active members of the labor force. They are not hospitalized behind the battle lines but are still at the front, taking part in the competitive struggle. Unemployment benefits have a distinct effect on the balance of power between employer and employee. Because of its close connection with the competitive market, unemployment insurance exhibits much of the heterogeneity of the wage structure, and this heterogeneity cannot be *assumed* to be undesirable.

"Better" is also assumed to mean "more liberal." This assumption, like the other, needs to be subjected to closer scrutiny than it has yet received. Obviously there must be some limit to liberality beyond which the more liberal is not the better. The proper norms for each provision of the law must be established before this assumption can be accorded full credence. Still, the following discussion will accept the assumption. After all, there is general agreement that the original provisions were not liberal enough, that the increase in liberality has been for the most part desirable, and that there is room for further liberalization of at least some provisions. This general agreement is strong enough to justify at least a provisional assumption—but only provisional and only an assumption—that more *is* better and permits us to discuss the issue of cost sharing in terms of its probable effect on program liberality.

Why are some states less liberal than others? Two principal reasons suggest themselves—states are unwilling or unable to be more liberal. In the former case the problem is not primarily financial, and the solution is not cost sharing but a set of federal standards. The issue of federal standards is distinct from the issue of cost sharing and will not be discussed here.[4]

Rather, we are concerned with states that are in some sense unable, though willing, to liberalize their programs. The argument assumes that if they receive a subsidy for part of their excess costs, they will further liberalize their programs. Presumably these states are considered unable because they carry a greater than average burden of unemployment or because they have less than average financial means.

Table 22 provides some data useful for estimating the extent of correlation between these two possible causes of lesser liberality and the actual degree of liberality manifested in the laws of the states.

[4] For a detailed analysis of the issue of a federal benefit standard, see Joseph M. Becker, *Unemployment Benefits: Should There Be a Compulsory Federal Standard?* (Washington, D.C.: American Enterprise Institute, 1980).

Although limited in many ways, the data serve as a first rough approximation to the desired information. They also serve as a reminder of the more refined correlation studies needed if an adequate case is ever to be built for cost sharing.[5]

Table 7 merely summarizes table 22 and classifies the states as above or below the national average. Both tables reflect a decade of recent experience, 1968–1977. Later data were not available at the time the tables were constructed, and earlier data would not be particularly relevant to the issue of current cost sharing. A comparison of the tables with figure 2, however, suggests that the relative position of most states, at least as regards their cost rates, has remained fairly stable over the life of the program.

Table 22 consists of three ratios that measure, respectively, costs, unemployment, and liberality. The first is the ratio of benefits to wages, a cost rate.[6] As a ratio, it automatically adjusts for state differences in size and wage levels. This cost rate is determined primarily by the insured unemployment rate (IUR), which is the ratio of claimants to covered employment.[7] This ratio automatically adjusts for differences in state size but not for differences in coverage. The cost rate is determined also by the liberality of a state law. Division of the cost rate by the insured unemployment rate removes most of the factor of unemployment and leaves principally the factor of liberality. This third ratio, a ratio of ratios, is usable as a liberality index, a measure of the relative liberality of state unemployment insurance programs.

The liberality index is limited in many ways, chiefly by the interdependence of some of its components. The IUR is determined not only by the number of the unemployed in a state but also by the liberality of a state's provisions. The more liberal a state's provisions, the higher will be its IUR, everything else being equal.[8] Since the

[5] In an unpublished paper, Raymond Munts has prepared a basically similar but more refined liberality index that permits comparison with table 22 for the years 1968-1972. The two indexes yield basically similar results. The differences are more frequent, as would be expected, near the mode of the distribution, where a relatively small change can move an item above or below the average.

[6] More specifically, it is the ratio of the average weekly benefit amount to the average weekly total wage.

[7] More specifically, it is the ratio of average weekly insured unemployment to average monthly covered employment.

[8] The effect of some of the provisions is direct and simple, whereas the effect of other provisions, for example, the proportion of covered employment to total employment, is indirect and complex. Also, some provisions have a greater effect on IUR than do others. For example, the provisions that determine benefit duration have a greater effect than the provisions that determine the benefit amount. They all, however, have the same general effect: The more liberal the provision, the higher the IUR.

TABLE 7

TABLE 7
LIBERALITY INDEX AND INSURED UNEMPLOYMENT RATE, 1968–1977, AND PER CAPITA INCOME, 1978

| | Liberality Index | | Insured Unemployment Rate | | Per Capita Income ($) | |
	Above average (1)	Below average (2)	Above average (3)	Below average (4)	Above average (5)	Below average (6)
Alabama		0.282		3.27		6,291
Alaska		0.249	7.85		10,963	
Arizona		0.279		2.87		7,372
Arkansas		0.276	3.73			5,969
California	0.311		4.55		8,927	
Colorado		0.298		1.64	8,105	
Connecticut	0.409		4.36		8,911	
Delaware	0.380			2.87	8,534	
District of Columbia	0.436			2.29	9,924	
Florida		0.253		2.29		7,573
Georgia		0.286		2.22		6,705
Hawaii	0.413		3.56		8,437	
Idaho		0.284	3.87			7,015
Illinois		0.306		3.01	8,903	
Indiana		0.262		2.31		7,706
Iowa	0.373			2.10	8,002	
Kansas	0.337			2.40	7,882	
Kentucky		0.295		3.19		6,607
Louisiana		0.307		3.25		6,716
Maine		0.304	5.13			6,292
Maryland	0.322			2.92	8,363	
Massachusetts	0.349		4.77		7,924	
Michigan		0.285	4.60		8,483	
Minnesota	0.339			2.77	7,910	
Mississippi		0.237		2.52		5,529
Missouri		0.259		3.29		7,313
Montana	0.313		3.83			6,755
Nebraska	0.339			1.88		7,582
Nevada	0.326		4.32		9,439	
New Hampshire	0.320			2.62		7,357
New Jersey	0.359		5.01		8,773	
New Mexico		0.251	3.60			6,574

(Table continues)

TABLE 7 (continued)

	Liberality Index		Insured Unemployment Rate		Per Capita Income ($)	
	Above average (1)	Below average (2)	Above average (3)	Below average (4)	Above average (5)	Below average (6)
New York		0.303	4.30		8,224	
North Carolina		0.291		2.57		6,575
North Dakota	0.346			3.11		7,174
Ohio	0.317			2.39	7,855	
Oklahoma		0.242		2.71		7,137
Oregon		0.273	4.67		8,092	
Pennsylvania	0.341		4.13			7,740
Puerto Rico		0.212	12.01			N.A.
Rhode Island	0.384		5.32			7,472
South Carolina		0.287		2.83		6,288
South Dakota		0.290		1.93		6,864
Tennessee		0.260		3.20		6,547
Texas		0.246		1.30		7,730
Utah	0.312			3.17		6,566
Vermont	0.343		4.66			6,566
Virginia	0.312			1.34		7,671
Washington		0.286	6.48		8,495	
West Virginia		0.214	3.67			6,624
Wisconsin	0.338			3.17		7,532
Wyoming		0.305		1.57	8,636	
Total	23	29	21	31	21	31

NOTES: N.A. = not available. For all states, average liberality index = 0.311, average uninsured employment rate = 3.49, and average per capita income = $7,836.

SOURCE: Table 22 for columns 1 through 4. U.S. Department of Commerce, *Survey of Current Business*, August 1979, part 2, p. 31, for columns 5 and 6.

divisor of the liberality index is thus larger than it would be if it measured only unemployment, the index itself is lower than it would be if it measured only the liberality of a state's provisions. Also, since this effect is greater as a state's provisions are more liberal, the difference in liberality between the states is somewhat larger than that shown in the table. This characteristic does not, however, impair the validity of the general argument based on the table.

In addition to this limitation, stemming from the arithmetic of the ratios, the basic data themselves have rough edges. Sources of error are varied; to take one example, the reporting of some of the states to the federal government shows too much variation to be entirely reliable. Because of such limitations, a highly refined analysis of the available data, especially where small differences are involved, would be of doubtful value. Hence the analysis is confined to a simple comparison of four groups of states classified as they are above or below the average in liberality and unemployment.

Group A: Above Average in Liberality, below Average in Unemployment

Delaware	Minnesota	Ohio
District of Columbia	Nebraska	Utah
Iowa	New Hampshire	Virginia
Kansas	North Dakota	Wisconsin
Maryland		

These thirteen states include about 19 percent of all covered employment. Of the thirteen, five are in the East, seven in the Midwest, and one in the West. This group offers little or nothing to support an argument for cost sharing; in their case the argument would have to proceed by a series of difficult steps. Since these states are already above average in liberality, the argument would first have to establish some absolute norm of adequacy (the most difficult step of all) and would then have to prove that these states were deficient by that norm; that they were deficient because of the cost burden (even though their costs are below average) and that the subsidy they would receive from a cost-sharing program (very small, if any, in their case) would induce them to increase the liberality of their program; and finally that the taxes imposed on other states to produce the funds received by these states would not cause the other states to reduce the liberality of their own programs.

Group B: Above Average in Both Liberality and Unemployment

California	Montana	Pennsylvania
Connecticut	Nevada	Rhode Island
Hawaii	New Jersey	Vermont
Massachusetts		

These ten states include about 26 percent of all covered employment. Six are in the East and four are in the West. Insofar as they are already above average in liberality, any argument for cost sharing would have to follow the same difficult path indicated for Group A.

Unlike Group A, however, Group B is above average in unemployment, and some of these states might hope to draw a significant subsidy from a cost-sharing fund. Would the subsidy affect the liberality of their programs? The answer depends on the extent to which cost, stemming from unemployment, acts as a deterrent to liberality.

Obviously other features besides cost enter into the determination of liberality. As may be seen in table 7, of the twenty-one states with above-average unemployment, half (the ten in Group B) are nevertheless above average in liberality. Although there is a common-sense plausibility to the argument that cost is a deterrent to liberality (if the cost is great enough, it certainly will affect liberality at some point), the shape of the function connecting cost with liberality is obscure.

Some of these states have incurred sizable debts (see table 2), and any subsidy received is as likely to be used to reduce their debts as to liberalize benefits. Although a subsidy is not likely to induce Group B states to increase the liberality of their programs, it could conceivably prevent them from reducing present liberality. The easiest way in which these states could deliberalize their programs would involve not increasing the maximum benefit as wages rose. But this easy way is out of reach for the Group B states. Nine of the ten (see table 2) use the device of the flexible maximum, which raises the maximum benefit automatically with wages. In sum, the effect of the subsidy on the liberality of Group B states is highly speculative, but it is certain that until the present the burden of unemployment has not prevented these states from having programs of above-average liberality.

Group C: Below Average in Both Liberality and Unemployment

Alabama	Indiana	Oklahoma
Arizona	Kentucky	South Carolina
Colorado	Louisiana	South Dakota
Florida	Mississippi	Tennessee
Georgia	Missouri	Texas
Illinois	North Carolina	Wyoming

These eighteen states include about 36 percent of covered employment. The group is predominantly located in the South and West. It includes no states from the Northeast and only four from the Midwest. Illinois should probably not be regarded as belonging to this group. In recent years Illinois has attained to more than average liberality and could now be properly included in Group A or B (most likely in Group A).

It is particularly difficult to establish a causal relationship between the degree of liberality and the burden of unemployment in the case of Group C states. Since these states already have below-average unemployment, there is no immediately evident reason for affirming that unemployment has kept them below the average in liberality. In any case, since these states are below average in unemployment, they would not draw significant amounts of subsidy from any cost-sharing plan that might be set up. For both reasons, Group C states do not provide clear evidence of the need for cost sharing.[9]

Group D: Below Average in Liberality, above Average in Unemployment

Alaska	Michigan	Puerto Rico
Arkansas	New Mexico	Washington
Idaho	New York	West Virginia
Maine	Oregon	

These eleven states include about 19 percent of the covered employment. Because they are above average in unemployment, they may receive significant help from a cost-sharing program; because they are below average in liberality, they may use the help to liberalize their programs. These are the states that provide the chief argument for cost sharing, for here, if anywhere, the burden of unemployment may be the cause of a low level of liberality. If the argument for cost sharing cannot be made effectively in the case of these states, it probably cannot be made anywhere.

Four states (Arkansas, Idaho, New Mexico, and West Virginia) had unemployment rates only slightly in excess of the national average and would have received very small grants, if any, if a cost-sharing plan had been in operation during the decade covered by the table. The smaller the grant, the less likely it is to have a significant effect on the state receiving it. Cost must compete with other, especially political, factors in determining the liberality of a state program; a small difference in cost is likely to be lost among other factors.

Of the remaining seven, the significance of New York must be largely discounted. The chief reason that New York is not more liberal does not relate to the cost of the program. New York labor

---

[9] Moreover, five of these states (Colorado, South Carolina, South Dakota, Tennessee, and Wyoming) are so close to the average in liberality that in the Munts index they are rated above average.

53

and management have been battling over experience rating, and the liberality of the program has been a victim of that struggle. The chief reason for the less than average liberality of the New York program is the low maximum benefit in that state. The New York senate, at the behest of management, has been unwilling to raise the maximum benefit until experience rating has been restored permanently. The New York assembly, at the behest of labor, has refused to accept this condition. Any grant that New York could have received in the past decade would not have changed the outcome of that political contest. On the other hand, without this stalemate, the maximum benefit would have been raised, and any increase in it would have put New York over the average in liberality, for it is only slightly below the average now. (In the Munts index, New York is rated above average in liberality.)

Of the six remaining states, two can justly be regarded as special cases. Alaska is below average in liberality primarily because it has a low maximum benefit, but this low maximum is the result of a federal regulation. Half of Alaska's claimants leave the state each winter and draw their benefits while living elsewhere. Because Alaska's wages and all other prices are so much higher than those in the other states, Alaska would like to distinguish between its two groups of claimants and pay higher benefits to claimants who remain in Alaska. Since this is forbidden by federal regulation, Alaska pays all claimants benefits that are suitable for the migrants. (If the state paid the migrants a benefit that equaled half their Alaskan wage, their benefit would equal or exceed available wages in the lower forty-eight states.) The solution here is not to pay grants to Alaska but to lift the federal regulation. The recent subsidies paid by the Alaskan government to all its citizens and the remission of their taxes should be sufficient indication that state taxes are not the primary problem here.

Puerto Rico is the other exceptional case. Its economy is completely dependent on that of the United States, and its unemployment insurance program is very different from the programs in the continental United States. In nearly every respect it must be considered separately from the other states.

Maine, Michigan, Oregon, and Washington, with 7.12 percent of covered employment, thus represent the only clear examples of states where above-average unemployment might be the cause of below-average liberality and where a subsidy might result in increased liberality. In addition it is relevant to note that Maine is the only one of these four states that is below average in per capita income (see table 7). Thus the argument for cost sharing applies to only a small part of the system and even there only as a possibility—note that I say "might be," "might result." Possibilities are insufficient when, as here, the argument must sustain the burden of proof.

Moreover, the case for Michigan is weakened by two considerations. Michigan is not a poor state but ranks well above the average in per capita income (table 7). Also, the auto industry and its subsidiaries explain the largest part of Michigan's above-average unemployment, and these industries in particular have been the most prosperous. They pay their workers well above the average of all workers. Even more to the point, most of them provide supplemental unemployment benefits that increase the protection of the regular program in both amount and duration of benefits. If Michigan employers can afford the cost of this additional protection, they should be able to afford the cost of regular unemployment benefits. Certainly employers in states that cannot afford these higher wages and supplemental benefits should not be asked to pay the cost of Michigan firms. Although the auto industry is currently having its difficulties, it will probably revive. In June 1980, a leading New York brokerage firm was strongly advising its clients to buy auto stocks. There have been times in the past when even General Motors was a "deficit employer," that is, drew more from the state unemployment insurance fund than it had contributed, but always the company has recovered and more than repaid the benefits its workers used. (Additional data on Michigan's performance are shown in table 5, which is based on tables 17 and 18).

The argument has sometimes been made that states with high costs, especially states in debt, must levy so high an average tax on their employers that there is no room for a meaningful tax differential among employers, that is, for experience rating. This is partially true. There is a limit to the tax that may be levied against the individual employer, a restriction imposed by both economic and political considerations. Given this limit at the top, the higher the average tax rises in a state, the more the lower tax ranks must move up, thus diminishing the difference between high-cost and low-cost employers. What this argument for cost sharing overlooks is that experience rating applies first to the states themselves. Diminishing the responsibility of each state to bear its own costs does not serve to defend the principle of experience rating.

Extrinsic Effects

Apart from effects on the unemployment insurance program itself, cost sharing is said to be justified for economic reasons. These economic considerations relate principally to the financial needs of states, the allocation of responsibility for unemployment, and interstate competition for industry.

Financial Need. A state may be considered unable to pay its own unemployment insurance costs not only because its burden is above average but also because its financial means are below average. As a measure of financial ability, table 7 shows the per capita income of each state for the year 1978. Although this is not an entirely satisfactory measure (it does not take into consideration, for example, differences in living costs), it roughly approximates the desired measure. It also serves, of course, as a reminder of the more refined data that proposals for cost sharing need to develop, since they bear the burden of proof.

In any system of cost sharing, the payees will likely be the states with above-average unemployment. In the decade covered by table 7, there were twenty-one such states, of whom eleven were above average in per capita income. The payers of the system will likely be the states with below-average unemployment. In the same decade, there were thirty-one such states, of whom twenty-one were also below average in per capita income. A cost-equalization scheme would require the twenty-one states with below-average income[10] to pay part of the costs of the eleven states with above-average income.[11]

The strongest argument for cost sharing can be made in the case of states that have three characteristics: (1) they are below average in liberality; hence there is probably room for increased liberality; (2) they are above average in unemployment; hence they may expect to receive some significant subsidy from a cost-sharing plan; and (3) they are below average in per capita income; hence they may need some assistance from more fortunate states. Only five states exhibit these three characteristics: Arkansas, Idaho, Maine, New Mexico, and West Virginia. Collectively they account for only 2.7 percent of all covered employment. All the other states are already above average in liberality or are below average in unemployment or are above average in per capita income. Finally, of these five states, only one (Maine) had an unemployment rate notably above the average.

[10] Alabama, Arizona, Florida, Georgia, Indiana, Kentucky, Louisiana, Mississippi, Missouri, Nebraska, New Hampshire, North Carolina, North Dakota, Oklahoma, South Carolina, South Dakota, Tennessee, Texas, Utah, Virginia, and Wisconsin.

[11] Alaska, California, Connecticut, Hawaii, Massachusetts, Michigan, Nevada, New Jersey, New York, Oregon, and Washington.

56

Responsibility for Unemployment. To be persuasive, the argument for cost sharing must absolve the states that experience heavy unemployment from responsibility for that unemployment. Two chief lines of argument are used for that purpose.

Natural disasters. One approach makes use of the analogy with natural disasters. Every society has a policy of helping members who are experiencing unusual difficulty. A common example is the aid that the federal government provides to disaster areas. States that are burdened by unusually heavy unemployment are like disaster areas, it is argued, and should qualify for disaster assistance. Unemployment is similar to a natural disaster in that it is beyond the control of the states. The state of Washington has more unemployment than the state of Texas because of its climate and its seasonal industries. No matter how hard it tried, Washington could not bring its unemployment down to the low level that Texas enjoys. Michigan will always have a high unemployment rate because it is in the nature of the auto industry to produce more than average unemployment. If the nation wants automobiles, as it does, then the nation's consumers, whose fluctuating demand causes the unemployment that marks auto production, should bear part of the cost of that unemployment. The state that assumes the function of producing the autos should not be burdened with the total cost.[12]

The argument above limps badly: Unemployment differs basically from so-called natural disasters. Unemployment benefits are among the regular costs of doing business. They are about as predictable as most other business costs and are as traceable to particular economic activities. A firm engaged in outside construction work expects to experience more unemployment than one engaged in inside construction and very much more than a firm engaged in the banking business. These differential costs are translated into differential prices of various kinds by the normal workings of the competitive market.

Although it is true that the people in Texas who wish to have the use of automobiles manufactured in Michigan should be ready to share in the cost of the unemployment benefits necessarily connected with the production of automobiles, it does not follow that this sharing may

---

[12] For example: "Cyclical fluctuations in state unemployment rates are national in origin. It is irrational and inequitable to require states to bear the costs of programs that are not under their control. In the short run, the responsibility for laying off an auto worker in Michigan lies more with the consumer who does not buy a car—wherever that consumer may be—than with the firm which lays off that worker." Staff report, Northeast-Midwest Institute, August 1978, p. vi.

best be achieved by having the employers of Texas pay a subsidy to the employers of Michigan. Normally the purchasers of automobiles find the cost included in the price they have to pay for automobiles. This is the customary way of allowing the market to allocate resources. Michigan, not Texas, is responsible for the costs of producing automobiles.

It is useful to note an ambiguity in the term "responsible." When a firm is said to be responsible for its own unemployment, we do not mean that the firm is in some way at fault, that the economic agent, firm or state, could and should have done something differently so as to avoid unemployment. The economic agent is responsible for unemployment only in the sense of paying for it as a regular cost of engaging in that kind of economic activity. The cost is brought home to the "responsible" party only in the sense that this cost, just like wages and other business costs, is allocated to its source and thus becomes a part of the price mechanism. Whether the economic agent could or could not have avoided the unemployment is irrelevant to the economic meaning of "responsibility."

The importance of this observation may be measured by the frequency with which cost sharing is justified by the simple statement that a given economic agent, state or employer, could not control the amount of unemployment accompanying its activities. Of all the arguments used for cost sharing, this is the one most often used, but used without perception that the issue at stake is acceptance or rejection of the market as the principal allocator of resources.

National causes. States should not be held responsible, it is argued, for unemployment that is traceable to "national" causes. Cyclical unemployment is the leading example, since by definition the business cycle is a broad, national phenomenon with causes outside the boundaries of any particular state. Another example is the unemployment resulting from actions of Congress or the president, such as the closing of military installations or the permitting of competition by foreign products. Such unemployment should not be the burden of a few particular states but should be financed, at least in part, by a tax levied on the total economy.

This line of argument is subject to severe limitations. The notion of "national cause" is hopelessly vague. Most of the legislation pouring out of Congress and most of the administrative regulations pouring from the executive agencies have an economic impact, and they are all national causes. No principle is available to identify national causes that do and do not absolve the states from responsibility for any resulting unemployment. When a federal installation is closed, some states are especially affected, but these are usually the same states that lobbied vigorously to obtain the installation in the first place and profited from it as long as it was in operation. There is no obvious principle by which to absolve such states from the cost of the resulting unemployment benefits.

Cyclical unemployment is as clearly linked with particular economic activities as are other kinds of unemployment. The cyclically unemployed are not a unique group. Their unemployment stems from the same complex mixture of personal and impersonal causes as unemployment in general. A business recession is merely a time when these causes are more operative than usual, that is, when a greater number of firms than usual are cutting back on economic activity.

The crucial point is that some kinds of economic activity are predictably more subject than others to cyclical swings. Firms engaged in such activities normally take this characteristic into account and plan accordingly. If the losses of cyclically sensitive industries are greater on the downswing, their profits are generally greater on the upswing. The cost of unemployment benefits is only a part, a small part, of the cyclical costs a firm expects to meet in its normal operations. Although somewhat less predictable than other kinds of unemployment benefits, and somewhat larger in amount, benefits paid under the provisions of the regular unemployment insurance system during a recession belong among the regular costs of doing business.[13]

Interstate competition. The argument for cost sharing derived from this source has generally emphasized the impact of interstate competition on the unemployment insurance program itself. In recent years, however, the emphasis has shifted somewhat to effects on the economy. For example, the lengthy document prepared by the Northeast-Midwest Institute argues for cost sharing primarily in terms of the economic needs of the Northeast and Midwest.[14]

For some years now, so the argument goes, there has been a flow of industry into the Sun Belt at the expense of the Snow Belt states. Although the trend cannot, and perhaps should not, be stopped, it

[13] The Bureau of Economic Analysis of the U.S. Department of Commerce has measured state sensitivity to cyclical swings over the five postwar cycles occurring during the period 1948-1973. The bureau computed state sensitivity indexes by measuring cyclical swings in nonfarm payrolls. The Division of Research and Statistics of the Ohio Bureau of Employment Services has published these indexes in the form of a chart (E-545) dated June 19, 1980 (Columbus, Ohio).

[14] Northeast-Midwest Institute, "The Crisis in Unemployment Insurance: A Regional Analysis," in U.S. Congress, House, Subcommittee on Public Assistance and Unemployment Compensation of the Committee on Ways and Means, *Hearings on H.R. 8291 and H.R. 8453,* August 10 and 11, 1978, pp. 53-107.

should not proceed at so fast a pace that great economic losses are sustained as factories and utilities are left to deteriorate in the North while new ones are built in the South. If the proposed program provided more help to the North than to the South, as it probably would, this result could be considered desirable insofar as it might slow the pace of the exodus. Although the amount of assistance provided is small, when the margin of profit is thin, as it is for the threatened industries, every little bit helps.

Although the states in the North would receive a disproportionate part of the subsidy, they are also the ones that pay a disproportionate part of the federal taxes. The present pattern of federal taxes and benefits still reflects the early, now rapidly changing pattern of income distribution whereby the North systematically subsidizes the South. The subsidy provided by current cost-sharing proposals would represent some repayment of a historic debt.

This argument has obvious validity, but it must be balanced by the observation that although the gap between North and South is narrowing, the northern states are still richer than those of the South and for that reason might be expected to meet their own unemployment insurance costs. There is not the same justification for subsidizing the North now that there was for subsidizing the South in an earlier generation. Instead, we seem to be approaching a more balanced situation in which each state may properly be required to meet its own costs.

The market, if allowed to work, will bring about needed adjustments. As the Federal Reserve Bank of Philadelphia noted:

> Change is in the wind. One notable change is that the cost of doing business in the South is rising faster than in the North. Wage differentials have narrowed considerably. The Sunbelt is paying for its prosperity much as the Northeast did earlier.
>
> Also, many of the industries that found it advantageous to develop elsewhere have already done so. Those that have stayed in older metropolitan centers have remained because they anticipate profitable operations in their present locations. The period of significant job relocation from North to South, therefore, may have passed.[15]

There could be a situation, of course, in which the cost of unemployment benefits for a particular state or industry was so great as to endanger the stability of the state or industry. In this case, it would

[15] Federal Reserve Bank of Philadelphia, *Business Review* (March/April 1979), p. 3.

be consonant with general practice for the federal government to provide—preferably directly rather than through the unemployment insurance program—a temporary subsidy that would carry the affected economic agents over the emergency. Still, evidence would have to be forthcoming that the tax burden was indeed "unbearable." The Brodhead and Javits bills propose the norm of 6 percent insured unemployment as the point at which unemployment costs become unbearable, but no evidence has been presented to establish this alleged fact.

The benefit-cost equivalent of a 6 percent insured unemployment rate is about 2 percent of total wages. When the program was first established in 1935, it was decided that given the weak state of the economy at that time, the average state tax rate should not exceed 3 percent of total wages. Since the economy now is much stronger than it was then, the question inevitably presents itself: Why are firms today unable to meet a tax rate above 2 percent of total wages? It may be said that there was no basis for the early estimate of 3 percent, and that is true. It is equally true, however, that no evidence has been adduced for the proposition that is the basis for current proposals for cost sharing, namely, that states are unable to levy a tax higher than 2 percent.

The argument that the unemployment insurance tax has a significant effect on the movement of firms into or out of a state, although often proposed, has never been supported by evidence. In fact, the available evidence runs counter to this proposition. The unemployment insurance tax is a small part of fringe benefits, a much smaller part of employee remuneration, and a still smaller part of total production costs. The leaders of management who have testified before Congress have all taken the position that the unemployment tax ranks far down the line of factors that influence the location of a firm.

A more refined argument would point out that although the unemployment insurance cost is small, it has some impact. Particularly as a proportion of profits, the unemployment insurance tax can be significant to the well-being of a firm, especially firms with small profit margins. In states that have declining industries, there may be many such firms, but when—and to what extent— should declining firms be aided? One function of the market, and an essential one, is to eliminate uneconomical activities. The burden of proof on proposals of assistance is heavy.

Conclusion

States are economic entities in competition with one another. Hence, other things being equal, each state is expected to meet its own costs.

In a society like ours, which uses the competitive market and the price system as its chief method for the allocation of resources among its citizens, the burden of proof rests on any proposal to have the federal government intervene in the competition between the states and to require the employers of one state to subsidize the employers of another. The difficulty of developing such proof no doubt accounts for its scarcity.

If we decide to intervene in the market on the basis of no stronger evidence than exists in this case, we have decided to accept a minimal commitment to the market. When values have been thus inverted, so that the market is expected to bear the burden of proof instead of enjoying the benefit of the doubt, many basic changes become possible. If circumstances such as those currently characterizing the unemployment insurance program can induce us to intervene, we may expect very many other sets of circumstances in the future to have a similar effect.

What is at stake also is the nature of the unemployment insurance program. Until the present it has been an extension of the wage system. To undertake change on the basis of no more compelling evidence of need than exists currently is to embark on a course leading to basic overhaul of the unemployment insurance system.

4

Experience Rating: Its Effect on Cost Allocation

Background

As I remarked earlier, the problem of distributing the burden of unemployment taxes has two parts, the distribution between states and the distribution between individual employers within a state. The first was the subject of the previous two chapters; the latter is the subject of the following three chapters.

Among the countries of the world, the United States is unique in its method of financing unemployment insurance. Where other countries usually draw funds from three sources (employers, employees, and government) and tax all employers uniformly, in the United States the program draws all its funds from a tax on employers and varies this tax according to the individual employer's experience with unemployment.[1] The system of levying the unemployment insurance tax in some relation to the individual employer's experience with unemployment is called experience rating. This chapter and chapter 5 seek to evaluate experience rating and to answer the question: Is experience rating a desirable method of allocating the tax burden among employers?

The issue has been very controversial. To some, especially organized labor, experience rating is the root of all that is wrong with unemployment insurance: Its strict allocation of costs acts as an undesirable limitation on benefits. To others, it is an essential part of a program that seeks to make unemployment benefits an extension of the wage system, a regular cost of doing business. The contro-

---

[1] No state uses general revenues. The District of Columbia did so briefly at the very beginning of the program, and the federal government does so, of course, for the coverage of government employees. In 1980 three states (Alabama, Alaska, and New Jersey) levied a small flat tax on employees in addition to the larger, experience-rated tax on employers. For an explanation of the mechanics of experience rating, see Joseph M. Becker, *Experience Rating in Unemployment Insurance* (Baltimore: Johns Hopkins University Press, 1972), pp. 366-70.

versy is closely connected with the still deeper issue of the function of the relative roles to be assigned to the competitive market and to government as the principal allocator of the nation's resources. It is probably this connection that explains why the experience-rating controversy carries such a high emotional voltage. As Edwin Witte remarked a decade after the main battle had been concluded: "Differences of opinion [on experience rating] among the champions of the institution [unemployment insurance] are so extreme as to disrupt lifelong friendships." [2]

Is experience rating desirable? The answer is to be found in a review of the major effects of experience rating, which are listed below as they relate to the economy or to the unemployment insurance program itself.

1. Allocation of social cost
4. Stabilization of employment } Effects on the economy
5. Countercyclical timing

2. Administration of unemployment insurance } Effects on unemployment insurance
3. Legislation in unemployment insurance

The numbers indicate the order of importance and the order in which they are considered in this and the following chapter. The second, third, and fourth effects can occur only to the extent that employers are motivated to do something or to refrain from doing something. The first and fifth effects, on the contrary, occur independently of employer awareness of experience rating. The basic effect is the allocation of costs: All the other effects can occur only to the extent that costs are allocated. The present chapter is taken up entirely with the allocation of costs; the following chapter deals with the remaining effects.

For information on the nature and extent of these effects, I examined several studies produced for the National Commission on Unemployment Compensation. One study attempts to measure the effect of experience rating on employer participation in administration, on employer efforts to stabilize employment, and on the allocation of costs (numbers 2, 4, and 1 in the list above).[3] This study, like

[2] Edwin E. Witte, "Development of Unemployment Compensation," *Yale Law Journal*, vol. 55, no. 1 (December 1945), p. 21.
[3] Terrence C. Halpin, *Three Essays on the Effect of Experience Rating in Unemployment Insurance*, Employment and Training Administration, U.S. Department of Labor, 1978.

many others prepared for the commission, utilizes an econometric approach and is more noteworthy for the ingenuity of its methods than for the practical usefulness of its findings. Although the study claims only to measure effects and expressly disavows evaluation, it somehow manages to conclude that experience rating "should be strengthened."

Another study seeks to establish the degree of probability that any given "industry" will be a subsidized or a subsidizing industry because of experience rating. The study's sixteen pages of tables are accompanied by a meager three-page analysis that adds little of use for our present purpose.[4]

A third study asks whether the federal government should use internal experience rating, that is, whether the government should charge each (federal) agency for the benefits drawn by that agency's employees rather than continue to lump together the experience of all agencies under one cost rate. The scope of the study is very limited. It seeks merely to compare the dollar expense of using internal experience rating with the dollar savings that might result. It has nothing to say about the other, more important, effects of experience rating.[5]

A fourth study reflects a wealth of practical experience in the unemployment insurance program. Still, it is useful primarily for constructing an effective experience-rating system rather than for judging the desirability of one.[6]

I refer to these recent studies where they are applicable, but in sum they do not contribute substantially to the evaluation of experience rating. For the most part I have had to rely on a study made of experience rating in 1972.[7] Where possible, I have added recent data—enough to show that the essential characteristics of the earlier experience still hold—but generally I have used data pertaining to the decade of the 1960s.

For our purpose, these earlier data are actually more useful than current data would be. Our objective is evaluation (is experience rating desirable or undesirable?), and for that purpose the decade of the 1960s is ideal. Current data, reflecting the severe recession of

---

[4] Raymond C. Munts and Ephraim Asher, "Cross-Subsidies among Industries from 1969 to 1978," *Unemployment Compensation: Studies and Research*, vol. 2, National Commission on Unemployment Compensation, July 1980, pp. 277-97.

[5] Booz-Allen and Hamilton, Inc., "The Feasibility of Alternative UCFE Chargeback Systems," *Unemployment Compensation: Studies and Research*, vol. 2, National Commission on Unemployment Compensation, July 1980, pp. 599-602.

[6] Russell L. Hibbard, "Solvency Measures and Experience Rating," *Unemployment Compensation: Studies and Research*, vol. 2, National Commission on Unemployment Compensation, July 1980, pp. 329-38.

[7] Becker, *Experience Rating*.

1974–1975, show an unusually high average tax rate and a consequently reduced range for the operation of experience rating. The 1960s, on the contrary, the longest period of prosperity in our history, show low average tax rates and a consequent expanded range for the operation of experience rating. As Aristotle has observed, the nature of anything may be observed most clearly in its most developed specimen. Since our interest is in the effects of experience rating, it follows that we can reach significant conclusions by concentrating on those situations where experience rating is most developed and its effects most pronounced. Here, if anywhere, the effects should be most visible.

Social Cost

The first effect of experience rating is to allocate more accurately the social cost associated with unemployment. The notion of social cost is currently in the forefront of public consciousness as economic activities that result in polluted air and water are required to bear more of the costs attendant on a polluted environment. The increased cost will lead, we hope, to decreased pollution. If it does not, however, society will at any rate have a more accurate measure of the real net value of the service or good produced. Similarly, economic activities that result in unemployment are required by experience rating to bear more of the cost of this form of social "pollution." The following quotation from Edwin Witte, the "father of social security," serves as an accurate summary of the key issue involved in the allocation effect of experience rating.

> Our private economy is grounded upon the concept that each industry should stand on its own feet. Honest cost accounting requires that all costs be ascertained and properly allocated to the commodities produced or services rendered. An industry which operates intermittently occasions great costs to its employees and to society through its methods of operation. *Whether it can or cannot operate more regularly,* the unemployment which arises by reason of its intermittent or irregular operation is a cost which should be charged to the establishment producing the goods or services and which gets the profits of the enterprise. Every reason that can be advanced for contributions from employers only—and in all but six states [three, in 1980] all contributions come from the employers—logically leads to variable contribution rates, rates adjusted to risk and costs. In a socialistic economy it might be proper to have all industry collectively bear the costs of unemployment;

in a private economy, where the profits go to particular entrepreneurs, all costs of production should be borne by the particular establishments, and these should include the unemployment compensation costs, as well as all other costs. [Italics added] [8]

A helpful illustration of the meaning of "responsibility" as applied to the allocation of social costs is at hand in the history of workmen's compensation. In Europe the development of this program proceeded in three stages. (1) It was recognized that the employer's responsibility extended to injured workmen in cases where it was the employer's fault and (a later development) that the burden of proof was on the employer to establish that the accident had occurred without any negligence on his (the employer's) part. (2) Accidents that happen through no one's fault but are the expected consequences of certain industrial processes are also the employer's responsibility. This became known as "trade risk" and became accepted as a regular cost of doing business, just as the repair of inanimate machinery was accepted as a regular cost of doing business. (3) Finally, the employer was held responsible for compensating for all injuries, even those caused by some negligence on the part of the employee.

The "responsibility" relevant to the allocative effect of experience rating includes responsibility for "trade risk." It may even include responsibility for unemployment traceable to employee action. Suppose, for example, that a state law provides benefits without disqualification to a claimant who quit his job for a compelling personal reason or that it provides benefits after a temporary disqualification to a claimant who was discharged for cause; if an employer chooses to do business in that state, he may then be considered to have assumed responsibility for this payment as a business cost, much as he does for costs occasioned by other state laws governing minimum wages, maximum hours, safety devices, and so forth.

This meaning of employer responsibility needs to be emphasized because it is often misunderstood, even after so many years. During the hearings held by the National Commission on Unemployment Compensation, witnesses repeatedly argued that particular states or particular industries should not be held accountable for the costs of unemployment connected with their operations because they were not "responsible" for the unemployment—that is, because the kind of economic activity in which they were engaged by its very nature generated higher than average unemployment. More than one of the

---

[8] Robert J. Lampman, ed., *Social Security Perspectives: Essays by Edwin E. Witte* (Madison: University of Wisconsin Press, 1962), pp. 274-75.

research papers prepared for the National Commission on Unemployment Compensation also reflects this incorrect view of the "responsibility" underlying experience rating. The historically correct view is that expressed in the Witte quotation, in which experience rating is understood to grow from the basic choice our society has made of the competitive market as our principal mechanism for allocating resources.

The suitability of experience rating as an allocator of resources depends on two conditions. First, the benefit-cost rates[9] of individual employers must differ substantially and predictably. Unless they differ substantially, it is not worthwhile to keep track of the differences; unless they differ predictably, that is, with some degree of regularity, their differences cannot properly be made the basis of an insurance system. Second, the tax rates[10] assigned to employers must have some regular relationship to cost rates. Given the fulfillment of these two conditions, experience rating makes sense for an economy that uses the market as its primary mechanism for the distribution of resources. The first obvious step is therefore to review the available data on cost rates and tax rates.

Cost Rates

The ideal data would be the cost rates of individual firms for the whole period during which each firm was in the program. Such data are desirable because only the individual firm has a pocketbook and pays taxes. Still, the few data that are available on the experience of individual firms are usually limited to a single year and do not permit us to follow the experience of the firm from one period to the next. Hence they do not reveal how regular (predictable) such experience may or may not be. To cast some light on the regularity of experience, it is usually necessary to make use of proxy data, chiefly averages by industry groups. These averages may be used only as approximations of the experience of the individual firms included in the classifications, for within each industry there are firms—many firms—whose individual experience differs appreciably from the average of the classification. It cannot be emphasized too strongly that the relevant differences are between high-cost and low-cost firms, no matter what the industry.

[9] Benefit-cost rates, often termed simply cost rates, are benefits expressed as a percentage of wages.
[10] Tax rates are taxes expressed as a percentage of wages.

Industry Groups. The eleven states in table 23 include about 45 percent of all covered employment and exemplify states of varying size, cost rates, geographical location, and type of experience-rating system. Considerable representative value therefore attaches to this sample. The eleven-year period 1957–1967 is long enough to allow fundamental economic differences to show through and includes two recessions and an extended period of prosperity. It is immediately evident that the average cost rates of the first three industrial divisions were appreciably higher, and that those of the last four industrial divisions were appreciably lower, than the state average for all industries. Manufacturing, the largest single division, was usually closest to the state average. Table 8 presents similar data for a recent year (1978) and shows that the general relationships still hold.

Industrywide averages conceal many large and regular differences, which appear when similar cost rates (eleven-year averages) are compiled for industries at the two-digit level.[11] At this level, "manufacturing" is seen to encompass a range of economic activities of widely differing cost rates. Apparel and textiles, for example, are consistently among the highest, whereas chemicals and printing are consistently among the lowest. In construction, the general contractors are found to have a cost rate double that of the contractors for special trades. All the industrial divisions exhibit the same phenomenon: The smaller the industrial classification, the greater the differences in cost rates. Presumably, the differences would be greatest at the level of the individual firm, the economically significant unit.

Individual Firms. A few states publish the cost rates of individual firms for single years. Table 9 illustrates such data for New York in 1967 and 1976. The distribution of cost rates in this table shows how the tax rates would have been distributed if the New York program had been completely experience rated. Some firms might be paying tax rates twenty times greater than those of other firms.

It is noteworthy that the great preponderance of firms and payrolls are in the low-cost category. This skewed distribution, typical of all states, has both an economic and a political significance. Since most of the payroll is in the low-cost firms, most of the system's income must come from these same firms, a necessity that limits the possible extent of experience rating. Further, most firms pay a lower

---

[11] For tables showing two-digit data, see Joseph M. Becker, S.J., *Experience Rating in Unemployment Insurance: Virtue or Vice* (Kalamazoo, Mich.: W. E. Upjohn Institute for Employment Research, 1972), pp. 16-17.

TABLE 8

Benefit-Cost Rates, Tax Rates, and Cost/Tax Ratios for Selected States, by Industry Division, 1978

Division	Calif.	Maine	Mass.	N.J.[a]	N.Y.	Ohio	Oreg.	Pa.	Utah	Va.	Wash.
All industry divisions											
Cost rate	2.6	2.6	1.8	N.A.	5.0	1.7	2.0	3.7	1.2	1.2	2.4
Tax rate	3.5	3.2	3.8	N.A.	3.4	2.8	2.2	3.2	1.7	1.2	3.0
Cost/tax ratio	74.1	81.1	47.4	110.1	145.6	61.2	89.3	115.5	67.2	103.8	79.8
Agriculture, forestry, and fisheries											
Cost rate	4.1	4.2	7.8	N.A.	—	3.3	3.2	5.0	—	2.9	5.9
Tax rate	3.7	3.4	5.4	N.A.	—	3.3	2.6	2.8	—	1.3	3.0
Cost/tax ratio	110.3	122.8	144.4	254.8	—	102.5	122.4	178.6	—	227.7	198.1
Mining, including quarrying											
Cost rate	1.7	17.9	5.3	N.A.	—	3.9	3.1	7.5	1.0	2.0	3.4
Tax rate	3.2	3.5	5.3	N.A.	—	2.7	2.5	3.0	1.7	0.9	3.0
Cost/tax ratio	53.1	515.9	100.0	135.9	—	145.8	124.2	249.6	59.8	214.5	112.1
Construction											
Cost rate	4.2	7.2	7.8	N.A.	18.8	6.9	3.8	11.4	2.9	2.9	4.4
Tax rate	4.3	4.1	5.9	N.A.	4.5	4.1	2.6	3.7	2.2	2.0	3.0
Cost/tax ratio	97.8	174.1	132.2	171.9	413.3	170.3	143.6	309.8	130.6	144.0	148.2
Manufacturing											
Cost rate	2.8	2.4	1.6	N.A.	5.2	1.6	2.4	3.0	1.0	1.2	2.4

Tax rate	3.7	3.3	3.7	N.A.	3.7	3.2	2.3	3.6	1.6	1.6	3.0
Cost/tax ratio	77.1	71.7	43.2	111.2	141.8	48.4	105.2	84.0	59.0	74.1	79.8
Transportation, communication, and utilities											
Cost rate	2.0	1.7	1.6	N.A.	3.1	1.3	1.1	2.4	0.7	0.6	1.6
Tax rate	2.9	2.8	3.5	N.A.	3.0	2.2	1.9	2.8	1.5	0.7	3.0
Cost/tax ratio	69.8	61.0	45.7	88.7	103.4	57.6	57.7	86.4	46.4	79.4	54.2
Wholesale and retail trade											
Cost rate	2.2	1.6	1.5	N.A.	4.0	0.9	1.4	3.3	0.9	0.5	2.3
Tax rate	3.3	2.9	3.4	N.A.	3.3	2.3	2.2	3.0	1.7	0.8	3.0
Cost/tax ratio	66.0	55.8	44.1	101.4	121.3	40.8	65.3	109.0	53.0	56.7	75.5
Finance, insurance, and real estate											
Cost rate	1.3	0.9	0.6	N.A.	2.5	0.4	0.9	1.3	0.6	0.3	1.3
Tax rate	2.9	2.6	3.1	N.A.	2.7	1.7	2.0	2.5	1.6	0.6	3.0
Cost/tax ratio	44.0	32.6	19.4	81.0	92.5	24.4	44.2	52.1	34.8	47.4	42.4
Services											
Cost rate	2.5	2.7	1.4	N.A.	4.7	1.1	1.5	2.9	1.3	0.7	2.0
Tax rate	3.5	3.2	3.8	N.A.	3.5	2.4	2.2	2.8	2.0	0.8	3.0
Cost/tax ratio	71.8	83.8	36.8	103.6	134.6	44.8	67.1	100.8	65.9	79.0	66.2

NOTE: N.A. = not available.

a Data are for 1939–1978 (cumulative), not for 1978.

SOURCE: E.S.-204 reports supplied by U.S. Department of Labor or by individual states.

TABLE 9
PERCENTAGE DISTRIBUTION OF FIRMS AND TAXABLE PAYROLLS BY BENEFIT-COST RATE, NEW YORK, 1967 AND 1976

Benefit-Cost Rate	1967		1976	
	Firms	Taxable payrolls	Firms	Taxable payrolls
Total	100.0	100.0	100.0	100.0
0.0– 0.5 [a]	71.5	46.0	56.2	17.4
0.5– 1.0 [a]	4.1	18.4	2.6	7.7
1.0– 1.5 [a]	3.0	8.6	2.4	9.5
1.5– 2.0 [a]	2.2	5.1	2.4	11.0
2.0– 4.0	5.9	11.8	7.6	23.4
4.0– 6.0	3.2	3.5	5.5	10.6
6.0– 8.0	2.1	2.0	4.0	6.4
8.0–10.0	1.5	1.3	3.0	3.4
10.0–12.0	1.1	0.9	2.4	2.3
12.0–14.0	0.9	0.6	1.9	1.5
14.0–16.0	0.7	0.4	1.5	1.2
16.0–18.0	0.6	0.4	1.2	0.9
18.0–20.0	0.5	0.2	1.0	0.8
20.0 or more	2.8	0.8	8.2	3.8

NOTE: Benefit-cost rates show benefit charges as percentage of taxable payrolls.

[a] Distributions of small percentages of negative-balance firms and their benefit-cost rates, included herein, have been estimated.

SOURCE: Actuarial Unit, Bureau of Research and Evaluation, Division of Research and Statistics, New York State.

tax under experience rating than they would if the tax were uniform. A part of the political appeal of experience rating derives from this large constituency of advantaged firms.

The Lesson of Cost Rates. The principal conclusion to be drawn from this historical pattern of cost rates is that it provides support for treating the cost of unemployment benefits as a regular cost of doing business. Like other business costs, the costs of unemployment benefits vary significantly and regularly with the types of economic activity with which they are associated. One can predict with a high degree of probability, for example, that in state after state, and year after year, the construction industry will draw much more from the fund per covered worker than will the industry division comprising finance, insurance, and real estate; that within construction, the special trades group will draw out less than will other groups; and that within the special trades, the electrical and plumbing groups will draw out much less than the painting and plastering groups. One can predict that costs in the service industries will be relatively greater than those in finance, insurance, and real estate, but smaller than those in manufacturing. One can predict that within manufacturing, heavy durables (for example, steel and autos) and seasonal activities (for example, canning and apparel) will draw out more per covered worker than will printing or chemicals or instruments. One can safely predict that within apparel manufacturing, benefit-cost rates in men's suits and women's undergarments will be relatively lower than those in hats or fur goods or women's outerwear.

The differences among the industry averages are clearly linked to the natures of the respective economic activities. Since the individual firms that compose the industry presumably share the economic nature of the industry, it may be inferred that the experience of most of the individual firms differs in somewhat the same way that the industry averages do. Most banks, for example, may be expected to have lower costs than do most construction firms. If eleven-year average cost rates could be obtained for individual firms, would the differences between firms be as large and as predictable as they are in the eleven-year averages for industry groups? The range of differences for individual firms would certainly be greater. The degree of stability (predictability) of the differences would certainly be less but would probably remain high. Most firms, in most years, can predict with considerable probability what next year's cost rate (not tax rate) will be.

To summarize, it is likely that individual firms' anticipated cost rates show great differences and that expectations are generally fulfilled. The existence of such significant and stable cost differences supports a preliminary conclusion that experience rating, unless it is objectionable for other reasons, is the appropriate arrangement for an economy in which the market is the principal instrument for the allocation of resources. On the other hand, since the individual firm cannot be certain that its own expectations will be fulfilled (for the competitive market poses an inescapable, constantly present risk), the use of the *insurance* technique is indicated. A combination of considerable risk with considerable predictability provides exactly the situation suitable for an insurance program financed through differentiated premiums.

Tax Rates

Although cost rates determine the potential degree of experience rating, the actual degree is determined by tax rates. All the effects that are attributed to experience rating depend upon the pattern of tax rates. The limits within which all the desirable and undesirable effects of experience rating can possibly occur are set by the degree of experience rating in the system, which in turn is determined by the pattern of tax rates. The larger and more regular the tax differentials, the more likely that experience rating has significant effects.

The most desirable data for the purpose of measuring regularity would be the tax rates of individual firms averaged over a long period of time. Although such data are nonexistent, a usable approximation may be found in the long-term average tax rates of industry groups, such as those shown in table 23.[12] The general picture conveyed by such data is one of predictable regularity. The "lesson of cost rates" applies generally to tax rates also. Table 8 provides confirmation of the "lesson": the relationships between the industries remained substantially unchanged ten years later, after the system had weathered the most severe financial strain in its history.

The significance of tax differentials produced by experience rating depends not only on their regularity but also on their size. A detailed view of tax differentials is provided in table 24 for 1967, a year of financial ease, and in table 10 for 1978, a year of financial stringency. As is clear, there has been a considerable dispersion of tax rates in most states in both years.

In 1967 about 40 percent of the taxable wages were at the lower end of the tax spectrum, whereas about 20 percent were at the upper end. The tax difference between these two groups averaged about 2 or 3 percent of taxable wages. In 1978 the distribution of tax rates was only slightly narrower than in 1967. The compression at the lower end of the scale was balanced by an expansion at the upper end. The entire scale had moved upward. The retention of this much experience rating in a period of financial stress is a striking indication of the vitality of experience rating. One would expect the states to move closer than they did to a uniform tax after almost half the states had exhausted their reserves and gone into debt.

How important are the tax differentials reflected in the tables 24 and 10? The answer must vary with the kind of firm (it is more important to a labor-intensive firm than to a capital-intensive firm)

---

12 Similar data are available for industries at the two- and three-digit levels. See Becker, *Experience Rating*, chap. 4.

TABLE 10

PERCENTAGE DISTRIBUTION OF TAXABLE WAGES OF ACTIVE ACCOUNTS ELIGIBLE FOR EXPERIENCE RATING, BY TAX RATE, 1978

Type of Plan	Employer Contribution Rate													
	0.0	0.1	0.2	0.3	0.4–0.5	0.6–0.9	1.0–1.8	1.9–2.6	2.7	2.71–3.1	3.2–3.5	3.6–3.9	4.0–4.4	4.5 and over
Reserve-ratio plan														
Arizona	0.0		1.1	0.0	0.4	1.0	24.6	35.1	3.8	7.8	14.6	11.6	0.0	0.0
Arkansas					7.2	7.5	42.1	14.3	2.3	14.2			12.4	
California				0.4			1.7	15.9	4.8	18.7	15.4	10.9	12.4	20.2
Colorado					0.2	5.2	79.5		0.9	5.3	3.3	5.3		
District of Columbia									100.0					
Georgia	3.5	0.4	0.5	0.7	1.2	8.4	40.4	24.2	0.4	4.3	8.9	0.8	2.0	4.3
Hawaii											100.0			
Idaho						9.1	38.3	27.4	16.4	1.5	2.9	2.9	1.5	
Indiana				19.3	4.2	15.3	20.2	14.8	2.4	11.4	12.4			
Iowa						14.3	23.8	14.4		4.7	4.8			
Kansas	4.8		4.8	4.8	4.8	4.8	4.8	4.8	4.8	4.8	4.8	4.8	4.8	28.5
Kentucky					3.0	32.7	7.2	11.8	3.9				4.8	37.6
Louisiana							6.5	20.6	31.2	10.3			9.9	4.1
Maine								41.6	4.5	16.4	11.8	6.8	2.7	16.2
Massachusetts								28.4	3.7	14.1	11.3	8.3	7.7	26.5
Missouri	8.4		0.1	0.1	0.1	1.5	41.9	24.8	6.9			16.2		

(Table continues)

75

TABLE 10 (continued)

Type of Plan	Employer Contribution Rate													
	0.0	0.1	0.2	0.3	0.4–0.5	0.6–0.9	1.0–1.8	1.9–2.6	2.7	2.71–3.1	3.2–3.5	3.6–3.9	4.0–4.4	4.5 and over
Montana										100.0				
Nebraska		6.9	7.1	20.6	17.0		11.8	5.7	24.2			6.7		
Nevada	0.7					0.2	5.4	37.9	31.9	24.6				
New Hampshire		0.7	2.1	1.5	3.8	7.5	24.7	38.9	5.4	5.5	2.4	1.6	2.0	3.1
New Jersey							18.6	16.5		4.4	6.0	4.3	13.5	36.7
New Mexico						30.8	47.6	8.3	2.5	1.3	0.7	1.1	7.7	
New York							11.6	15.7	2.2	8.1	6.3	19.1	17.7	19.3
North Carolina		5.7	0.8	0.6	2.1	3.9	23.6	26.5	27.7	2.4	1.7	1.6	0.6	2.8
North Dakota					7.3	9.2	27.0	21.9	21.2				13.4	
Ohio							36.7	23.7		8.5	4.6	3.8	3.7	23.8
Rhode Island								40.1	5.7	18.3	16.9	6.9	10.1	
South Carolina							39.0	24.2	31.6	3.6	0.7	0.2	0.7	
South Dakota	9.7	5.8	11.0	16.0	16.0	21.0	7.0	3.1	2.3			3.9		4.1
Tennessee				6.9	4.1	12.1	22.5	10.0	36.6	1.2	0.9	1.6	3.6	
West Virginia[a]				2.5	0.7	4.5	12.4	27.7	38.3	4.9	8.9			
Wisconsin	15.7					6.4	20.3	15.1		10.0	9.7	1.9	5.4	15.5
Benefit-wage-ratio plan														
Alabama							39.7	16.1		6.8	4.2	2.8	30.4	
Delaware		13.3	23.9	6.0	8.7	9.0	11.8	4.8	2.1	2.4	4.4	1.2	1.3	10.9
Illinois							12.7	7.1		4.2	3.2	3.2	69.1	

Oklahoma					52.6	3.9	7.6	4.0	0.8	10.2	1.6	1.0	1.5	16.8
Virginia	20.6	3.4	5.5	8.2	9.6	14.9	14.4	5.8	0.3	2.2	15.1			
Benefit-ratio plan														
Connecticut							38.9	19.0	1.5	4.6	4.1	4.0	3.7	24.2
Florida							25.8	17.4	2.0	5.4	4.8	4.3	4.5	35.8
Maryland		17.0	2.8	3.7	7.3	18.2	22.1	9.4	0.6	3.4	1.6	1.1	1.0	11.8
Michigan							10.6	17.1	1.5	5.5	5.3	4.1	9.7	46.2
Minnesota							54.6	17.6	2.0	4.1	3.0	2.4	2.8	13.7
Mississippi								59.4	40.6					
Oregon								10.0	5.0	20.0	23.0	33.0	9.0	
Pennsylvania							12.4	15.9		8.2	6.2	4.3	48.6	
Texas		32.6	16.1	13.2	13.2	10.6	9.7	2.4	0.1	0.6	0.4	0.4	0.2	
Vermont							30.4	26.2		8.6	4.4	4.3	8.8	17.3
Wyoming	25.5				43.6	13.0	4.3	7.4	6.2					
Payroll-variation plan														
Alaska								9.8		10.2	19.9		20.0	40.1
Utah							78.1	20.0	1.4	0.6				
Washington											100.0			

NOTE: Totals may not equal 100 percent because of rounding. The Louisiana data are obviously defective but could not be corrected.
[a] The data for West Virginia refer to employer accounts, not to taxable wages.
SOURCE: E.S.-204 reports supplied by U.S. Department of Labor or by individual states.

and with the profitability of the firm (it is more important to a firm with a low profit rate). The answer must vary especially with the different effects of experience rating. A differential that might be too small to affect the location of a firm might be large enough to affect a firm's employment policy, and a differential that might be too small to affect a firm's employment policy might be large enough to affect a firm's participation in unemployment insurance administration.[13]

It is evident that the tax differential produced by experience rating is not normally a major item of cost. It is also evident, on the other hand, that the tax is not a negligible cost item. It belongs to that multitude of small costs whose total a firm tries earnestly to control because in sum they affect the firm's position in competition with other firms in the industry and in competition with other industries for the consumer's dollar.

It is common for the financial officer of a company to want to know the cost of a proposed action in terms of unemployment insurance taxes. It may be that there is thought of closing a plant or store or that a decision has to be made between working the entire labor force part time or laying off some employees and working the rest full time. In contract negotiations it frequently happens that the unemployment insurance unit is called upon to supply an estimate of the unemployment benefit cost of agreeing to certain demands of the union with respect to pensions, holidays, pregnancies, layoffs, or vacations. Some firms set up a centralized unemployment insurance unit to control claims, others hire service companies to perform this function, and a few even apply experience rating internally—all indications that the size of the tax is of some importance to employers. Another clear indication is to be found in the battles that occur in the legislature between representatives of the various industries over the distribution of the total tax burden.

For two decades the federal government refused to cover its own employees under unemployment insurance; most state and local governments did not cover their employees until recently, when required to do so by the Congress. The reluctance of governments to assume the burden of the unemployment insurance tax is particularly eloquent testimony to its economic significance.

---

[13] For the effects on administration and stabilization, another type of calculation is appropriate. For these important effects, the significant comparison is between the total benefits payable to a claimant, which may amount to several thousand dollars, and the cost of doing whatever will make unnecessary the payment of benefits to that particular employee. In discussions of the impact of experience rating, this crucial relationship is frequently overlooked.

Cost/Tax Ratios

The potential for experience rating has not been fully realized. To the extent that experience rating is operative, the long-run cost/tax ratio of each firm will approach unity. To the extent that the ratios depart from unity, except for the cost of building reserves, experience rating is not fully operative. When industry averages depart from unity, it may be inferred that some firms in the industries with below-average ratios are subsidizing some firms in the industries with above-average ratios.

To judge from table 23, which shows eleven-year averages by major industry divisions, the program worked to produce a predictable redistribution of the tax burden in favor of the first three industry divisions in the table at the expense of the last four. It would be correct to say, for example, that firms in the (low-wage) retail trade industry have been subsidizing firms in the (high-wage) construction industry. Table 8 indicates that the same general relationships perdured through a period of severe recession.

Within these major industry divisions, there were even larger cost/tax discrepancies. Within manufacturing, for example, which as a whole approached unity, the apparel group had a cost/tax ratio of 223 (it took out more than two dollars for every dollar it contributed), whereas the printing group had a cost/tax ratio of only 64 (it took out only sixty-four cents for every dollar it contributed).[14]

Actually, the low-cost firms in all industries subsidize the high-cost firms in all industries, but the proportion of low-cost and high-cost firms among the various industries varies in predictable patterns. It is in this sense that one may think of the industries of finance and retail trade, for example, as subsidizing the industries of construction and apparel manufacturing.

Noncharged Benefits. One explanation for cost/tax discrepancies is to be found in the extent of noncharged benefits. Practically all states provide that in some circumstances the benefits paid will not be charged to the account of any individual employer. Most often the purpose of the provision is to reduce employer opposition to a particular kind of benefit—for example, a benefit paid to a claimant who has quit the job or benefits paid after twenty-six weeks. At issue is the definition of employer "responsibility" discussed above. The nar-

---

[14] These data and much additional information on cost/tax ratios may be found in Becker, *Experience Rating*, chaps. 4, 5.

rower the definition of employer responsibility, the more room there is for noncharging.

Noncharging would seem to countervene the federal law that a state may reduce the tax on an employer only by reason of that employer's favorable "experience" with unemployment. But the U.S. Department of Labor has tended, at least since 1944, to interpret this restriction loosely and to favor the spread of noncharging as an aid to liberalization of the program, especially of the disqualification provisions. Noncharging is favored also by employer service companies, which regularly list noncharged benefits as a saving that they have achieved for their clients.

The states differ greatly in their use of the noncharging device. In 1978, the various states noncharged the percent of total benefits indicated in table 11.[15] Eight states noncharged 30 percent or more of all benefits paid: Arkansas, Colorado, Connecticut (the highest), Idaho, Kansas, Maine, Mississippi, and Texas. At the other extreme, three states (Illinois, Michigan, and Wisconsin) noncharged no benefits, and five others (District of Columbia, Indiana, Iowa, New York, and North Dakota) noncharged less than 5 percent. The eight states that noncharged about a third of all benefits and the eight states that noncharged less than 5 percent evidently had very different concepts of the meaning of employer responsibility and the value of experience rating. In general, the more industrialized states tended to make less use of noncharging and hence greater use of experience rating. As noted below, noncharging explains why in some states a very small proportion of benefits is ineffectively charged.

Ineffectively Charged Benefits. A second reason why cost/tax ratios depart from unity is to be found in the extent to which benefits have been ineffectively charged. Specifically, we are concerned here with benefits charged against an employer whose reserve is exhausted and who is already paying the maximum tax. These benefits are charged ineffectively in the sense that they neither draw on accumulated past taxes (reserves) nor trigger additional current taxes. A rough impression of the outside extent of such benefits may be gained from the proportion of taxable payrolls taxed at the maximum (tables 24 and 10). Some of these payrolls are ineffectively taxed. In tables 23 and 8, also, the extent to which these cost/tax ratios exceed unity

---

[15] Noncharging relates only to states that use benefits or benefit derivatives as the base for tax rates. Excluded from the table, therefore, are Alaska, Utah, and Washington, which use the payroll-decline method of experience rating. Additional historical data on the practice of noncharging may be found in Becker, *Experience Rating*, pp. 102-9.

TABLE 11
Noncharged Benefits as a Percentage of Total Benefits, by State, 1978

State	Percentage	State	Percentage
Alabama	12	Montana	c
Alaska	a	Nebraska	25
Arizona	21	Nevada	5
Arkansas	37	New Hampshire	8
California	10	New Jersey	17
Colorado	36	New Mexico	23
Connecticut	41	New York [b]	1
Delaware [b]	14	North Carolina [b]	16
District of Columbia	1	North Dakota	2
Florida	17	Ohio	7
Georgia [b]	24	Oklahoma [b]	14
Hawaii [b]	25	Oregon [b]	24
Idaho	33	Pennsylvania	21
Illinois [b]	0	Rhode Island	7
Indiana	1	South Carolina	25
Iowa	3	South Dakota [b]	21
Kansas	39	Tennessee	d
Kentucky	12	Texas [b]	37
Louisiana	8	Utah	a
Maine	30	Vermont	29
Maryland	13	Virginia	8
Massachusetts	13	Washington	a
Michigan [b]	0	West Virginia	24
Minnesota	23	Wisconsin [b]	0
Mississippi	32	Wyoming	19
Missouri	27		

[a] Payroll variation plan.

[b] Data are for 1977 (Georgia, Hawaii, Illinois, Michigan, New York, North Carolina, Oklahoma, Oregon, South Dakota, Texas, Wisconsin), or for 1976 (Delaware).

[c] Experience rating temporarily suspended.

[d] No data available.

Source: Unemployment Insurance Service, U.S. Department of Labor.

is probably an indication of some benefits ineffectively charged. Thus in Massachusetts perhaps half the benefits paid to employees in the construction industry may have been ineffectively charged.

Table 25 offers a view of negative-balance firms (those that have drawn out more than they have paid in) in a few selected states for the year 1967. California serves to illustrate the use of the table. Reading from the top down, we may see that about a fifth (18 percent) of all firms in California were not paying their way. Many of these seem to have been small firms, since their payrolls accounted for only 14.2 percent of all payrolls. Yet these negative firms accounted for over half (51.8 percent) of all the benefits charged in the state that year. Of all the benefits charged in California that year, 28.0 percent were ineffectively charged, that is, were not matched by either the current contributions or the past contributions (reserves) of the relevant firms. Over half (53.9 percent) of all the benefits charged to California's negative firms were ineffectively charged, that is, the contributions of these firms covered only 46.1 percent of the benefits charged to them. In order to pay their way, these negative firms would have had to pay an *additional* average tax of 3.9 percent. During that period, employees of these negative firms drew out $2.17 for every dollar the firms contributed to the fund. Finally, 12.1 percent of the benefits paid by California in that period were not charged to any employer account.

Items 9 and 5 combined lead to the conclusion that in California about 40.1 percent of all benefits were paid outside the experience-rating mechanism—12.1 percent noncharged and 28.0 percent ineffectively charged. By the same measure—the sum of items 5 and 9—Michigan and Ohio had the highest degrees of experience rating, whereas Massachusetts and South Carolina had the lowest. South Carolina's very low proportion of ineffectively charged benefits must be interpreted in conjunction with its very high proportion of noncharged benefits. When nearly half the total benefits are not charged against individual accounts, it is to be expected that fewer individual accounts will show a negative balance.

Item 3 shows how large a proportion of the benefit flow is attributable to negative firms. In New York, for example, although negative firms accounted for only 14.9 percent of all firms and 13.8 percent of all payrolls, they accounted for 61.6 percent of all benefits. In prosperous periods the experience of the total program tends to be influenced greatly, even dominated, by the experience of negative firms. In 1967, negative firms made up only 10.6 percent of all firms in reserve-ratio states and accounted for only 7.1 percent of all payrolls; yet they accounted for 40.6 percent of all benefits charged.

Table 12 shows similar data for a more recent year. The five items of the table correspond to items 1, 2, 3, 5, and 9 of table 25 but relate to 1978. Table 12 leads to two observations: the degree of experience rating had diminished by 1978, but it was still substantial, and in six states, a greater proportion of benefits was noncharged

TABLE 12

Significant Measures Relating to Negative-Balance Firms, Selected States, 1978

Measure	Calif.	Mass.	Mich.	N.J.	N.Y.	Ohio	Pa.	S.C.	Wis.
1. Firms with negative balances as a percentage of all firms	15.7	22.7	32.1	34.0	26.0	16.0	22.9	6.8	15.2
2. Taxable payrolls of firms with negative balances as a percentage of all taxable payrolls	14.3	13.1	28.0	35.6	28.4	29.9	19.2	11.0	14.4
3. Benefits charged to negative-balance firms as a percentage of all benefits charged to all firms	52.5	46.0	68.1	65.2	72.7	58.1	N.A.	N.A.	26.9
4. Deficit[a] of negative-balance firms as a percentage of all benefits charged to all firms	22.7	17.0	26.3	20.7[b]	42.5	30.3	24.9	N.A.	N.A.
5. Noncharged benefits as a percentage of all benefits paid	9.6	20.3	16.1	7.1	1.9	7.2	21.0	24.9	6.85

NOTE: N.A. = not available.

[a] Deficit = excess of benefits charged to negative-balance firms over their contributions, including any subsidiary taxes.

[b] Cumulative from 1939 through 1978.

SOURCE: Data supplied by the agency as requested.

than in the earlier period. The latter is a particularly significant development, reflecting as it does a departure in principle from experience rating. In six states (California, Massachusetts, Michigan, New York, Ohio, and Pennsylvania) about a third or more of all benefits were outside the scope of experience rating (sum of items 4 and 5).

A decline in experience rating was especially noticeable in Michigan and Ohio, probably the result of the heavy cutbacks in autos and related industries. In other states, less affected by the decline in durable manufacturing, the decline in experience rating was less marked. In general, after the most severe recession in the program's history, experience rating was still affecting more than two-thirds of all benefits paid.

Table 13 throws some additional light on the degree of experience rating in recent years. Fragmentary though they are, these data represent the best view available. The main limitations on experience rating are shown in the first three columns (ineffectively charged benefits, benefits charged to firms that have ceased to exist, and non-charged benefits) and are summed in the last column. For example, in Arizona the proportion of benefits falling outside the operation of experience rating was 26.1 percent. Obviously, for these fourteen states in this period the full potential of experience rating was far from being actualized. The period described in the table was, of course, one of unusually heavy benefit outlays; in a more ordinary period the proportion of ineffectively charged benefits (column 1) would be smaller. Also, the proportion of employers who escape the control of experience rating is much smaller than the proportion of benefits thus affected. This is because the socialized benefits are usually heavily concentrated among a few firms.

It is often objected that the states are not free in the matter of experience rating, that they are forced to adopt experience rating if they wish to levy an average state tax less than the federal tax against which the state tax is to be offset. Although this is correct technically, in practice the statement means little. Any state may have as little experience rating as it wishes, even when its average tax rate is below the federal tax. First, a state may adopt a form of experience rating, like payroll variation, that minimizes all the more controversial effects of experience rating. Second, whatever the form of experience rating, the state may arrange its tax schedule so as to group all taxpayers in a few classes (for example, Washington in table 24 or Mississippi in table 10). Finally, a state may make wide use of noncharging or ineffectively charging benefits (for example, South Carolina or New York in tables 25 and 12).

TABLE 13

PERCENTAGE OF BENEFITS SOCIALIZED, SELECTED STATES, AVERAGE 1971–1978

State	Net Percentage Charged to Negative Balances[a] (1)	Percentage Charged to Inactive Accounts (2)	Percentage Noncharged (3)	Total Percentage Socialized (4)
Arizona	−3.2	5.3	24.0	26.1
California[b]	30.9	0.6	8.7	40.3
Hawaii[b]	22.9	8.2	19.4	50.4
Idaho	15.4	2.7	27.6	45.7
Iowa[c]	18.5	7.7	5.8	31.9
Kentucky	24.4	6.3	11.3	42.0
Michigan[d]	21.0	5.5	N.A.	N.A.
Nebraska[e]	22.1	0.9	27.3	50.2
New Jersey	23.7	7.0	10.1	40.8
New Mexico	14.8	10.6	24.7	50.1
New York	43.5	7.1	1.3	51.9
North Carolina	10.1	6.4	14.7	31.2
North Dakota	33.8	6.6	4.3	44.7
South Carolina[f]	8.9	7.0	35.9	51.8

NOTE: N.A. = not available.

[a] Benefits charged against employers with negative balances minus taxes paid by such employers.

[b] Most data are for five years, 1974-1978.

[c] Most data are for two years, 1977-1978.

[d] Most data are for seven years, 1971-1977.

[e] Most data are for seven years, 1972-1978.

[f] Most data are for five years, 1971-1975.

SOURCE: *The Unemployment Benefit Advisor*, February 3, 1981, table 1.

In fact, the states have freely chosen to incorporate a high degree of experience rating in their laws. Most states (thirty-two in 1980) have chosen the reserve-ratio system of experience rating, which achieves the most exact accounting of individual employer experience and is most likely to produce all the effects, good or bad, expected of experience rating. The states have levied maximum tax rates much above the federally mandated maximum. They have also levied very low, even zero, tax rates so as to allow a significant spread of differentiated rates. In general, states are not compelled against their desires to adopt experience rating; rather, they adopt a degree of experience rating greater than the law requires and usually greater than their federal partner likes to see.

Objections to Allocative Effect

Experience rating is sometimes charged with putting a crushing tax burden on certain types of firms, especially those that are small, seasonal, or declining. The relationship between experience rating and *small firms* may be summed up in three propositions.[16] (1) Since the great majority of small firms have a tax rate below the state average tax, they would be burdened with a heavier rate under a uniform tax than they are under experience rating. (2) The smallest firms predominate among the subsidized, whereas the largest firms predominate among the subsidizers. (3) The tax rates of small firms are subject to greater fluctuations under experience rating than they would be under a uniform tax. Although small firms as a group cluster at the lower end of the tax spectrum, individual firms may move very quickly to the upper end.[17]

Experience rating is also charged with imposing too great a burden on *seasonal firms*. The issue here is not whether the employees of seasonal firms should receive unemployment benefits, but only which firms should pay for the benefits. It is argued that if seasonal firms are required to pay more of their own costs, their activity will be curtailed, and they will provide less employment. The relationship of unemployment insurance to highly seasonal firms has always been a thorny problem, and there is no general solution. Each state must decide for itself in the light of its own total economic and political situation how to pay for the unemployment created by its seasonal firms.[18] In general, the states have not allowed the market to work freely but have so limited the maximum tax that seasonal firms enjoy substantial subsidies. When a subsidy becomes permanent, its economic rationality becomes suspect.

Finally, experience rating is said to impose too heavy a burden on *declining firms*. If a firm's payroll is declining because the

16 Detailed data supporting these propositions will be found in Becker, *Experience Rating*, chaps. 4, 5.

17 Several states have offered their small firms the choice of being grouped in a common tax account. The small firms declined with thanks, each preferring to keep its generally low, if volatile, individual account.

18 By 1980 New York had given preferential treatment to three of its industries: canning, garment, and construction. Whereas firms in other industries must face a possible 5.5 percent tax rate, these firms may not be taxed beyond a 3.2 percent rate.

demand for its product is shrinking, this criticism has considerable merit. A burden that a healthy man carries easily is onerous for an ailing man. On the other hand, the general good is not always, or even usually, served by prolonging the existence of a dying firm. Circumstances of time and place are decisive.

Why do state legislatures continue to allow the subsidization of one industry by another even when it means that a low-wage industry is subsidizing a high-wage industry? Ultimately and logically it implies a lack of trust in the market. More immediately and practically, it reflects the legislative process in a democracy, in which the demands of competing interest groups must somehow be balanced by legislators bent on satisfying constituents in the immediate present. As viewed by the legislature, the strain on practical politics resulting from an attempt to distribute the unemployment insurance tax burden more logically may not be worth the effort. If the program is meeting its essential financial obligations (is solvent), the legislature, having only limited time to find answers to an almost unlimited number of problems, may decide to follow one of the oldest of political guidelines and let sleeping dogs lie. Unemployment insurance will probably not be the only operation in the state that is not completely logical by economic norms. On the other hand, the degree of experience rating that the state legislatures have maintained in their programs, especially by steadily raising the maximum tax rate, shows that the legislators are not completely indifferent to economic logic.

5

Other Effects of Experience Rating

Of the four remaining effects of experience rating, two concern the unemployment insurance program itself (effects on administration and legislation) and two the economy (effects on employment stabilization and the business cycle). The effects on the unemployment insurance program are the more important for the evaluation of experience rating because they are both larger and more certain than the effects on the economy. The order in which the four are considered reflects the order of their importance.

Administration

The administration of a given law is almost as important as the law itself in determining who does and does not receive benefits. Experience rating provides a financial incentive for employers to participate in the administration of unemployment insurance and thus to influence the award or denial of benefits. This effect of experience rating is probably decisive for friend and foe alike. One praises or condemns experience rating largely as one favors or deplores this effect.

Recent data on this effect are sparse. In 1978, the U.S. Department of Labor commissioned an econometric analysis of the correlation between degrees of experience rating and employer activity in appealing claims.[1] The study's conclusion, that experience rating does increase employer participation, confirms existing knowledge but otherwise does not add much that is useful for policy-making purposes. The following analysis is based chiefly on three chapters of an earlier study.[2] The employer is called upon to participate at every stage of the claims process. He has a function to perform at the initial claim, when the employee first applies, at each continued claim, and in all

[1] Terrence C. Halpin, *Three Essays on the Effect of Experience Rating in Unemployment Insurance*, prepared for the U.S. Department of Labor, 1978.

[2] Joseph M. Becker, *Experience Rating in Unemployment Insurance* (Baltimore: Johns Hopkins University Press, 1972), chaps. 6, 7, 8.

appealed claims, whether the appeal is initiated by the employer or by the employee.

A proper appreciation of the dimensions of the employer's task is essential for understanding the role played by experience rating in inducing the employer to undertake the task. Employer participation in administration is not simple. It requires the maintenance of records more detailed than are needed for other personnel needs. The employer must keep records that will enable him to distinguish between literally dozens of different kinds of separation from employment and to prove the distinction if challenged.

Effective participation requires not merely adequate record keeping but also a knowledge of the unemployment insurance law. Some state associations of employers and a few large corporations have compiled manuals of instruction for the use of the technicians assigned to the task of handling unemployment insurance claims. Next to seeing the technician actually at work, the reading of these manuals is probably the most direct way in which one not familiar with the subject can understand the proposition that to participate in the administration of unemployment insurance is not a simple task: It requires adequate records, skilled personnel, and careful attention (that is, sufficient time). This proposition holds at every level of administration, but it acquires significance as a dispute over a claim mounts from the deputy to the referee to the board of review and finally to the courts.

In evaluating the effect of experience rating on administration, the usual two questions need to be answered: What is the extent of the effect, and is the effect desirable? Of the two, the second is the more important but also the more difficult to answer.

Extent of the Effect. The possible extent depends on the degree of experience rating, which varies considerably among the states. The extent of the effect also depends on the kind of participation required of employers. The degree of experience rating sufficient to induce participation at the level of the initial claim might not be sufficient to induce participation at the more difficult level of the appealed claim. The finding by Halpin of a correlation at the appeal stage constitutes an a fortiori argument for correlation at the earlier stages.

When there has been little experience rating, there has usually been little employer participation. During the reconversion period after World War II, the local unemployment insurance offices were paying benefits to veterans (under the Readjustment Act) as well as to claimants in the regular program. Although under the law employers had the same duties regarding both classes of claimants, employers generally ignored the veterans' claims, which were charged not against the employer but against the federal government.[3]

Employers paying the maximum tax rate have less of an incentive to protest or appeal claims, and agency personnel regularly report less activity on the part of such employers.[4] Some firms have adopted internal experience rating because they found their cost centers ignoring the burdensome task of participating in unemployment insurance administration.[5]

A study of internal experience rating for the federal government found that the U.S. Postal Service, to which internal experience rating had been applied, participated much more than did the other federal agencies, whose unemployment insurance costs were paid out of a general fund.[6]

> The USPS is much more active in the appeals process, initiating 20 percent of its lower level appeals and providing personal testimony in 51 percent of its appeals as compared to all other agencies which initiated no appeals and provided personal testimony in less than 1 percent of their lower level appeals brought by claimants.[7]

This is striking evidence that lessened employer participation accompanies lessened experience rating.

The potential inherent in experience rating appears most clearly in the case of firms that actualize that potential most fully. Table 14 shows the operations of the unemployment insurance unit of North American Rockwell Corporation (NR) during the period 1955–1970. The NR system of claims control was as developed as any I encountered in a year's survey of such systems and may be taken as an example of employer activity at the upper limit.

In the table, column 2 shows the growth of the company through 1964 and then its subsequent decline; in 1970 monthly employment was less than half its peak figure. The next three columns show the claims that arose during this employment history and the proportion of claims that the company protested. Column 8 shows

---

[3] Joseph M. Becker, S.J., *The Problem of Abuse in Unemployment Benefits* (New York: Columbia University Press, 1953), passim.

[4] Becker, *Experience Rating*, p. 149.

[5] Ibid., chap. 12.

[6] Booz-Allen and Hamilton, Inc., "The Feasibility of Alternative UCFE Chargeback Systems," *Unemployment Compensation: Studies and Research*, vol. 2 (Washington, D.C.: National Commission on Unemployment Compensation, July 1980), pp. 599-602.

[7] Ibid., p. 600.

the proportion of protested claims decided in favor of the company. The table reflects a large and effective operation. On the average, 37.5 percent of all claims were protested, and 82.3 percent of these protests were upheld.

The operations of the unemployment insurance unit responded sensitively to the underlying economic realities. The unusually high percentages of claims protested in 1955 and 1956 reflect a period when employment was building rapidly. Separations from employment were mostly discharges for misconduct or voluntary quits without good cause; therefore nearly all claims were protestable. Layoffs began in 1957, but the company was still able to offer employees who were laid off transfers to suitable work in other divisions; hence it was in a position to protest claims arising from the layoffs success-fully. In 1958, however, when layoffs were very heavy and alternative suitable work was not available, the percentage of claims protested was only 26.9. During the extraordinarily heavy layoffs of 1969–1970, the percentage of claims protested dropped still further to 10.5. This impression of a reasonable and responsible policy on the part of the unemployment insurance unit is confirmed by a win ratio that was above 80 percent in all but four years, when it declined slightly to about 75 percent.

The state's initial determination of a benefit claim may be appealed by either the claimant or the employer, at either the referee level or the board level. The central unemployment insurance unit of NR had the responsibility of representing the company at all appeal hearings. After the state had set a date for the hearing of the appeal, the unemployment insurance unit made the necessary preparations, which usually involved gathering more detailed information and presenting it in a more formal fashion than was needed for the determination at the initial level. Photostats of essential documents were prepared, affidavits were secured, and arrangements were made to have present at the hearing witnesses who could speak from first-hand knowledge ("percipient witnesses"). At the hearing itself, one of the staff of the unemployment insurance unit represented the company.

The company's activity was impressive at the appeal level also, where the cost of activity is much higher. During the period 1955–1970, the company appealed 22.1 percent of its protested claims and of these won 67.7 percent. Claimants appealed twice as many claims but won only 15 percent of their appeals, that is, the company won 85 percent of the time. In all appeals activity—employer and employee appeals combined—the employer position was confirmed 80 percent of the time. The company always appeared at the hearing when it was

TABLE 14

NORTH AMERICAN ROCKWELL CORPORATION, AEROSPACE AND
SYSTEMS GROUP, CLAIMS PROTESTED AT INITIAL DETERMINATION,
1955–1970

Fiscal Year (1)	Monthly Employment (2)	All Claims (3)	Claims Protested		No Determination Issued[a] (6)	Determinations Favorable to Employer	
			Number (4)	Percentage of all claims (5)		Number (7)	Percentage of all determinations[b] (8)
1955	46,136	2,773	2,263	81.6	216	1,893	92.5
1956	53,369	2,052	1,727	84.2	309	1,300	91.7
1957	49,722	2,668	2,012	75.4	359	1,468	88.8

Year							
1958	42,269	13,440	3,617	26.9	471	2,713	86.2
1959	50,717	4,599	1,457	31.7	234	1,009	82.5
1960	56,474	6,138	2,421	39.4	270	1,618	75.2
1961	67,630	6,679	3,594	53.8	341	2,457	75.5
1962	80,074	7,102	3,903	55.0	405	2,503	71.6
1963	87,949	10,419	5,305	50.9	596	3,609	76.6
1964	89,282	10,922	4,813	44.1	521	3,683	85.8
1965	85,262	10,956	4,671	42.6	591	3,502	85.8
1966	75,622	7,234	3,084	42.6	425	2,302	86.6
1967	74,168	7,220	2,846	39.4	316	2,137	84.5
1968	68,314	7,290	2,576	35.3	278	1,919	83.5
1969	54,920	11,879	2,419	20.4	222	1,751	79.7
1970	40,253	18,173	1,910	10.5	119	1,490	83.2
1955–70	1,022,161	129,544	48,618	37.5	5,673	35,354	82.3

a These are claims where the claimant received no benefits either because he had insufficient wage credits or because he did not report back to the local office after filing his initial claim.

b All determinations equal column 4 minus column 6.

Source: Data supplied by North American Rockwell Corporation.

the appellant, whereas claimants failed to appear 18 percent of the time when they were the appellants.[8]

The unemployment insurance unit classified protests according to the situation that occasioned the protest. Arranged in descending order of the size of the benefit charges involved, the eighteen kinds of situations were as follows:

Discharges or permitted
   resignations
Retirement
Forced medical leave
Other employment
Geographic move to
   join spouse
Personal reasons or personal
   illness
Overstayed leave or absence
   of five days
Transportation difficulties

Illness in family
Untimely answer to claim notice
Unsatisfactory probationary
   employee
Medical restrictions
Need for child care
Dissatisfaction with job or shift
Maternity leave
Military service
School (summer employees)
Employer misstatement

This list of possible sources of claims illustrates the complexity of the employment relationship and the consequent complexity of the task of controlling claims.

Several conclusions are reasonably clear from the experience of NR. First, this company considered claims control important, for it set up a control unit of five highly trained people. Second, this interest in claims control stemmed largely from experience rating. (The unit claimed to have saved the company over $12 million.) Third, if one may judge from the company's high win ratio at the levels of both initial protests and later appeals, the participation of this firm in the administrative process probably helped in the attainment of the objectives of the law. This impression was strengthened by interviews that I conducted with some of the deputies in the state local offices with whom the company's unemployment insurance unit frequently dealt. The deputies reported that the members of the firm's unemployment insurance unit seemed to be concerned to bring out all the facts needed for a proper decision but not to prevent the payment of benefits due under the law.

In states with a considerable degree of experience rating, the ratio of employer appeals to employee appeals is 1 to 3 or 4, but in states with a minimum degree of experience rating, such as Rhode Island,

---

[8] For additional tables and a more detailed analysis of employer activity at the appeal level, see Becker, *Experience Rating*, pp. 180-85.

Utah, or Washington, employers file very few appeals, less than one-tenth the number filed by employees.[9] In Rhode Island from 1958 to 1979 employer appeals were further discouraged by a requirement that an employer appellant pay a twenty-five-dollar fee, which the state retained unless the employer won his appeal.

Desirability of the Effect. Although there is little doubt that experience rating has a significant impact on employer participation in administration, there is considerable debate as to whether such a result is desirable. Presumably the norm of desirability is whether employer participation helps or hinders those charged with the administration of the law in the performance of their duty. The further question, whether the law itself is desirable, is a separate issue. Here the issue is merely whether, under a given law, employer participation helps or hinders the administration of the law.

As a first step toward evaluating employer participation in the administrative process, a questionnaire was sent in 1969 to a representative sample of experienced deputies and referees. These are the persons who are in constant contact with claimant and employer, serving as a bridge between them and arbitrating their disputes about claims—day after day, year after year. If any persons in the program have an opinion worth listening to, it would seem to be the deputies and referees. So this most knowledgeable group was asked the question: *Does employer participation in the administrative process help or hinder you in your job of carrying out the unemployment insurance law of your state?* All but one of the thirteen items in the questionnaire asked this central question in one form or another.

The questionnaire was restricted to respondents with five years' or more experience. In five years' time, deputies or referees would have become well trained, and extremists would have been weeded out. The questionnaire was sent to experienced deputies and referees in seventeen states: California, Maine, Massachusetts, Michigan, Mississippi, New York, Ohio, Oregon, Pennsylvania, Texas, Utah, Virginia, Washington, Wisconsin, and States A, B, and C.[10]

These seventeen states included over 60 percent of all covered employees and were broadly representative in point of size, geographical location, and type of experience-rating plan. The sample included eight large states, six small states, and three average-sized states. It included five states from the East, four from the Midwest,

---

[9] Employment and Training Administration, U.S. Department of Labor, *Unemployment Insurance Statistics*.

[10] Three states that participated in the survey preferred not to be identified.

four from the West, and four from the South. It also included the following experience-rating systems: reserve ratio (9), benefit ratio (4), benefit-wage ratio (2), and payroll variation (2). Ninety-one percent of the questionnaires were answered and returned. As an aid to the interpretation of the responses received in the questionnaire, I conducted follow-up interviews with deputies and referees in California, Massachusetts, Michigan, Utah, and State B. In these interviews I repeated the survey questions and probed for possible misunderstandings.

Respondents to the questionnaire were answering from a situation in which experience rating was actually operating, and the questionnaire provided them with the opportunity to reflect the prevalence or absence of the chief abuses usually attributed to experience rating, such as the filing of frivolous protests. No more was expected of the questionnaire than that it would narrow the limits within which the answers lay and would enable one to conclude that the extent of undesirable effects associated with experience rating might be as great as X but could not be greater than was compatible with Y. The degree to which the reaction of the respondents was in general unfavorable to employer participation would set the X limit, and the extent to which their reaction was favorable would set the Y limit.

Answers were classified as favorable, unfavorable, or neutral to employer participation. Responses that included any negative element at all were classified as unfavorable. The only responses that were classified as favorable were those that were clearly such. The remainder were classified as neutral. Although of the neutral answers none could reasonably be considered unfavorable, some could reasonably have been classified as favorable. Thus to the extent that there is bias in the classification, it is in the direction of minimizing the favorable vote and maximizing the unfavorable vote.

Despite this bias, the general impact of the responses was clearly favorable to employer participation. Speaking from a situation in which experience rating was operative, an overwhelming majority of these respondents nevertheless considered employer participation helpful to their task of administering the unemployment insurance law. The 13,067 answers received from 1,499 respondents were distributed as follows:

Response	Percent
Favorable to employer participation	74.0
Unfavorable to employer participation	15.0
Neutral	11.0

It should be noted that those percentages do not refer to employer actions or to the number of respondents; they refer only to the number of responses. It would not be correct, for example, to say that 15 percent of employer actions were judged unfavorably, or that 15 percent of the respondents passed an unfavorable judgment on employers. The correct statement is that 15 percent of all the answers received represented an unfavorable judgment. When presented with the opportunity to disapprove of employer actions, the deputies and referees did so 15 percent of the time. On the other hand, when presented with the opportunity to express approval of employer actions, they did so 74 percent of the time.

One question asked the opinion of the respondents on the specific charge that employers harassed claimants by filing "frivolous" protests and appeals. Of the respondents, one-fifth reported that this happened often (meaning in 10–20 percent of disputed claims), whereas one-half reported that it happened seldom (meaning in less than 5 percent of disputed claims). Subsequent interviews with the respondents revealed that many of them had given "frivolous" a wide meaning, so as to embrace all "useless" protests, including those stemming from simple ignorance of the law.

A special study made of Massachusetts's experience[11] provided a clearer answer to this somewhat ambiguous question for at least this one state. During the five-year period 1963–1967, the outside possible limit of employer harassment in Massachusetts would seem to have been much less than 1 percent of initial claims and an even tinier fraction of all claims. This was the proportion of claims challenged by the employer that were not challenged also by the state independently of the employer and that did not result in disqualification.

Over half (57.5 percent) of all respondents wanted more employer participation, whereas 15.1 percent expressed their general satisfaction with the existing situation. Only 4.8 percent expressed a wish for less employer participation, and even this low proportion chiefly reflected the answers in one state (State B). The most frequently expressed desires for changes in employer participation were that employers would provide more detailed information in their original protests, that they would appear at the hearings initiated by claimants, and that they would bring to all hearings, whether initiated by themselves or by claimants, "percipient witnesses," that is, those persons who could give firsthand testimony regarding the issues involved in the appeal.

---

[11] Becker, *Experience Rating*, chap. 7.

In the judgment of the program's deputies and referees, the gains from employer participation clearly outweighed the losses. If this judgment is correct, and if the original assumption is also correct—that experience rating promotes employer participation—then it would seem that the effect of experience rating on administration should be entered on the plus side when making up the balance sheet of the desirable and undesirable effects of experience rating.[12]

Legislation

As so often happens, the more important values are the more difficult to measure. The effect of experience rating on legislation is more important, potentially, than its effect on administration but is less important actually because so little is known of either its extent or its desirability. There is no efficient way to measure its extent and no convincing norm by which to judge its desirability. The best that can be done is to examine some probabilities.[13]

As one way of exploring these probabilities, a questionnaire was sent to forty-five very experienced persons in the ranks of management, government, and labor asking for their judgment on this issue. In various ways they were asked whether experience rating induced employers to participate more, and more effectively, in the legislative processes affecting experience rating. The following opinions reflect the returns from the questionnaire.

Extent of the Effect. It is likely that experience rating has some effect on disqualification provisions. As compared with a uniform employer tax, experience rating fosters greater employer interest in disqualifications, an interest likely to be translated into legislative action. Disqualification provisions in most states are probably somewhat stricter than they would have been if the employer tax had always been uniform.

It is doubtful whether experience rating has any significant direct influence on benefit amount or duration. The table below shows how various groups of employers might be expected to view any proposal to amend the law and increase benefit costs. The table shows under which tax system, uniform or experience rated, an employer would

[12] Halpin, *Three Essays,* reaches the conclusion that experience rating should be increased (p. 111) but does not attempt to offer any evidence for this normative proposition (p. 15). As far as I am aware, the only serious test of the desirability of this effect of experience rating is still the 1969 questionnaire mentioned in the text.

[13] For a fuller treatment of this effect, see Becker, *Experience Rating,* chap. 9.

see himself incurring the greater cost as the result of such an amendment.[14] The answers given purport to show not how his costs would actually be affected but only how he would expect them to be affected. Presumably his financial incentive to oppose a given legislative proposal will be in some proportion to the increase in his cost as he sees it.

To an employer whose long-term tax rate under experience rating is:	*The cost of increasing benefits appears greater under a tax system that is:*
A. At the minimum	uniform
B. Above the minimum but below the state average	uniform
C. Above the state average but below the maximum	experience rated
D. At the maximum	uniform

Under a uniform tax system, Class D employers would pay the average increase in taxes produced by a benefit liberalization, but under experience rating they would pay none of such increase because they would be already paying the maximum. Hence they should have less reason to oppose such a liberalization under experience rating than under a uniform tax. Indeed, as several of the respondents noted, they might welcome such a liberalization as a costless way of supplementing wages or maintaining a surplus work force. The same logic holds for some of the employers in Class A; namely, those whose long-term cost rate is well below the minimum tax rate. These employers also are in a "zone of indifference" to increased benefit costs.

The other employers in Class A, as well as all employers in Class B, would anticipate some increase in their costs under experience rating, but the increase would be less than under a uniform tax. Under experience rating they would pay for only their below-average share of the increased costs, whereas under a uniform tax they would pay the average share, which would include part of the above-average costs of other employers.

Only Class C employers would see the proposed liberalization as more costly for them under an experience-rated system than under a uniform tax system. Under a uniform tax, part of the increased costs attributable to the employees of Class C employers would be

14 This is not the same as showing which employers would be better off under which system. Obviously, classes A and B would be better off under experience rating, and classes C and D would be better off under a uniform tax.

borne by Class A and Class B employers, whereas under an experience-rated system, Class C employers would have to meet all—or at least more—of their own above-average costs. Class C as a proportion of all employers in a state varies from state to state and from time to time. On the average, perhaps about one-third of all employers are Class C employers.

According to this logic, a proposal to effect a given liberalization of the program would represent a greater cost to more employers under a uniform system of taxation than under experience rating. Under a uniform tax, all employers have a financial reason to oppose a liberalizing amendment; under experience rating, some employers have little or no financial reason to be in opposition. Hence if costs were the only factor influencing the attitude of employers, there should be more employers opposing a given liberalization under a uniform tax than under experience rating.

Does this logic work in fact? At the extremes—among the Class A and Class D employers—it clearly does in many cases. It is not uncommon to find that banks and construction companies, for example, are relatively indifferent—for opposite reasons—to unemployment insurance legislation, even when amendments are proposed that would increase the state average tax. Nearly all professional legislative representatives of employers report encounters with this kind of behavior. The logic is probably less operative for Class B and Class C employers, who usually do not understand the mechanism of the unemployment insurance tax well enough, or do not reflect on it enough, to be influenced by the logic involved.

Finally, in considering the extent of this effect, it may be well to glance briefly at two arguments that, though spurious, are often advanced. The first has to do with the total amount of money available for unemployment insurance purposes. It has often been alleged that experience rating results in an inadequate legislative program because it results in inadequate financing of the program. This argument is without basis. A reserve fund of any desired size can be achieved equally well by a uniform or an experience-rated tax. The forces that limit the size of these funds would be operative under a uniform tax as well as under experience rating, and the size of the funds would probably be about the same under either system.[15]

A second misleading issue involves interstate competition. Experience rating is alleged to intensify the competition among states for the location of firms, and this competition is said to limit the liberality

[15] This proposition is explained at length in Becker, *Experience Rating,* chaps. 2, 9.

of unemployment insurance provisions. The observations about inter-state competition made in earlier chapters apply here also. In addition, it should be noted that experience rating apparently decreases inter-state competition if it has any effect.[16]

In all the preceding discussion of effects, a crucial distinction must be kept in view. We are comparing, not a tax on employers and some other source of revenue, for example, general revenue, but two kinds of employer taxes, uniform and experience-rated. Some of the legislative effects attributed to experience rating may really stem from a more fundamental feature of the program, the limitation of the tax to employers. The exact question at issue is: What effects flow from an experience-rated tax that would not result from any tax levied on employers?

Desirability of the Effect. If one assumes that experience rating has at least some effect on at least some provisions of the law, a further question then arises: Is this effect desirable? In attempting to evaluate the desirability of employer participation in administration, an objective norm was available in the unemployment insurance law itself. "Desirability" could be given a meaningful definition in terms of whether employer participation helped or hindered in the attainment of the objectives of the law. But here the issue is the desirability of the law itself. What norms are available for evaluating whatever effect experience rating may have on the law?

At this level, the only available norms are the systems of social values, only once removed from the absolute values of philosophy and theology, upon which each society builds its social structures. Among these social values, the one most relevant is probably that placed on the competitive market as the primary instrument for the allocation of society's resources. Earlier observations about this value are relevant here.

How liberal can unemployment insurance be made without causing unemployment? How liberal can unemployment insurance be made without inviting attempts to obtain benefits illegally, with resulting loss of the program's reputation and of public support? These are the two principal limits on program liberalization, and our knowledge regarding both is sparse. In recent years a number of studies of the effect of unemployment insurance on the level of unemployment reached the conclusion that unemployment benefits increased the level to some degree.[17] Still, the smallness of the impact

[16] Ibid., p. 214.

[17] For a review of this literature, see Daniel S. Hamermesh, *Jobless Pay and the Economy* (Baltimore: Johns Hopkins University Press, 1977), pp. 31-58;

and the uncertainty attaching to the evidence keep these studies from having much significance for policy making. With respect to over-payments (illegal payments), the National Commission on Unemployment Compensation attempted to measure their extent, but with little success. The findings of the million-dollar study permitted widely differing estimates: Overpayments were as little as 3 percent or as much as 33 percent of all payments.[18] The logic of the study gives validity to either figure as a national estimate.

Given the lack of information on the two limits, one's decision as to when benefit liberalization begins to exceed the limits depends largely on how one allocates the benefit of the doubt and the burden of proof between the needs of the individual and the requirements of the competitive market. In any case, the matter is less important because, outside the area of disqualifications, experience rating probably has little effect on unemployment legislation.

Employment Stabilization

Desirability of the Effect. Society's first concern with unemployment must always be with its prevention. Unemployment is a disease of the body economic and, like any disease, should be prevented or cured if at all possible. Only unemployment that cannot be prevented or cured should be treated with the palliative of unemployment benefits. In its positive form, the goal of unemployment prevention is called employment stabilization. Thus in early 1935 President Roosevelt said, in his message to Congress transmitting the report of his Committee on Economic Security, "An unemployment compensation system should be constructed in such a way as to afford every practicable aid and incentive toward the larger purpose of employment stabilization." However expressed, this goal has been adopted formally by practically all the states. The typical state unemployment insurance law states that one of the objectives of the law is the stabilization of employment or the prevention of unemployment.

In itself, an unemployment insurance program may *increase* unemployment. Employees may be slower to return to work and, more important, employers may be less interested in managing their personnel policies so as to minimize unemployment. The latter

also see entries under Frank Brechling and Martin Feldstein in National Commission on Unemployment Compensation, *Unemployment Insurance: An Annotated Bibliography*, 1980.

18 Paul L. Burgess and Jerry L. Kingston, "Estimating Overpayments and Improper Payments in the Unemployment Insurance Program," *Unemployment Compensation: Studies and Research*, vol. 2 (Washington, D.C.: National Commission on Unemployment Compensation, July 1980), pp. 487-526.

danger was the one that most concerned Sir William Beveridge when he came to review the first two decades of the world's first unemployment insurance program. After a detailed analysis of the danger, he concluded: "Industries practising casual engagement or perpetual short time may settle down to batten on the taxation of other industries or of the general public in place of reforming their ways."[19] It was this danger that led Beveridge to consider the adoption of experience rating in order that unemployment insurance might not induce management to accept unemployment but might become an additional reason to avoid it.[20]

Experience rating is related to the goal of employment stabilization through three of its effects—on the allocation of resources, on the business cycle, and on the policies of management. The first effect was discussed in chapter 4, whereas the effect on the business cycle is discussed later in this chapter. This section of the chapter is devoted solely to the management effect; that is, the incentive that experience rating provides to the manager of a firm to avoid layoffs.

The management effect of experience rating was emphasized more in the early years than in later years, when its limitations became clearer. Some writers incorrectly suggest that in the early years this was the dominant and almost exclusive effect claimed for experience rating. Yet from the very beginning the allocation of costs was seen to be the dominant effect of experience rating, so that even if the system had no effect at all on employment stabilization, it would still be desirable as an allocator of social costs.[21] Still, the potential effect of experience rating on employment stabilization has always been important. In this case, the issue turns not on the effect's desirability (it is desirable) but only on its extent.

Extent of the Effect. Four studies have attempted to measure the management effect of experience rating.[22] The first two analyses used

[19] William H. Beveridge, *The Past and Present of Unemployment Insurance* (London: Oxford University Press, 1930), p. 43.

[20] William H. Beveridge, *Unemployment: A Problem of Industry* (London: Longmans, Green & Co., 1909 and 1930), p. 411.

[21] Becker, *Experience Rating*, p. 52.

[22] Charles A. Myers, *Employment Stabilization and the Wisconsin Act*, Bureau of Employment Security Memorandum, no. 10 (Washington, D.C., September 1940), and Myers, "Employment Stabilization and the Wisconsin Act," *American Economic Review*, vol. 29, no. 4 (December 1939); William H. Andrews, Jr., and Taulman A. Miller, *Employment Security Financing in Indiana* (Bloomington: Indiana University, School of Business, Bureau of Business Research, 1956); *Merit Rating*, Report of the State Advisory Council on Employment Security (Hartford: Connecticut Employment Security Division, January 1969); and Halpin, *Three Essays*.

interviews with employers, whose answers were checked against statistics for employment, man-hours, and labor turnover. The third used a questionnaire followed by interviews, and the fourth used an econometric approach.

The findings of the three earlier studies were generally similar. About a quarter of the firms surveyed (having about one-third of the covered employees) reported being influenced to some appreciable degree by the incentive of experience rating. Among the remaining firms, some were affected by the incentive to a slight degree, but the majority were not affected at all—either because they were already stable or because the cost of stabilization would have outweighed any gain from lower unemployment insurance taxes. The fourth study examined three industries (construction, apparel, and wood products) to see if their seasonal fluctuations were less in states with a higher degree of experience rating. It seemed to find such a correlation in the case of the apparel industry.

Experience rating ranks well below other forces making for employment stabilization because most unemployment insurance costs are not within the control of the individual firm. Most layoffs are occasioned by such uncontrollable economic forces as cyclical fluctuations, shifts (seasonal or secular) in consumer demand, changes in the technology of production, labor disputes, and interruptions in the supply of materials. The constant differences in unemployment costs among industries (chapter 4) are attributable to basic industrial differences that are independent of managerial motivation and skills.

The individual employer's incentive to control his unemployment insurance costs is further restricted by limits on experience rating. As shown, the unemployment insurance tax system is far from completely experience rated. If, for example, the construction industry were taxed its full costs, it would have to increase its prices or stabilize its employment patterns or both; the tax would be sufficient to induce change. If the garment industry of New York were taxed to pay its full unemployment insurance costs, parts of the industry would have to stabilize employment further or go out of business.

Not all unemployment is beyond the control of the individual firm, and not all stabilization policies are too costly. There remain areas within which the personnel and production policies adopted by management make for a lower net cost, especially if unemployment insurance costs are correctly calculated. The correct method of calculation varies with the different systems of experience rating but is basically simple in the most prevalent form, the reserve-ratio system. For all employers except those who are at the maximum and expect to remain there indefinitely, the following is a simple, workable rule:

Every benefit dollar charged against firm A's account will have to be replaced by a tax dollar from firm A.[23]

The following is one of many possible examples of such a calculation.

> Within the concept of a flexible labor pool, one company completely retained surplus, semi-skilled female assemblers for clerical positions, where a shortage existed. The costs of retraining were considerably less than the $1,300 in unemployment insurance benefits each laid-off employee could have expected to draw against the company account.[24]

Likewise, the true cost to a firm of hiring a temporary employee is the sum of the wages plus the unemployment benefits paid to the employee. If, for example, a worker received $800 in wages and then drew $400 in unemployment benefits, his true cost to the firm would be $1,200. Calculated on a per hour basis, the employee would have been paid for time and a half. The argument that it is desirable to have more rapid turnover of employees in order to share the unemployment—a practice that experience rating inhibits—has been answered many times, beginning as far back as 1940.[25]

The significance of the unemployment insurance tax is to be sought in its relationship, not to total operating costs, but to profits. Businessmen tend to think of taxes as "coming off the top of profits." In many instances, the dollar amount represented by the unemployment insurance tax is a significant proportion of profits. At my request, a half-dozen large firms in durable manufacturing calculated their unemployment insurance taxes as a proportion of profits (after taxes) for the decade 1960–1970. The proportions ranged from 3 percent to 7 percent. No company would consider negligible a cost that lowered its profits by 3 percent or 7 percent. Applied to profits of millions of dollars, these percentages represent large sums. In any given year, some firms find that the unemployment insurance tax is larger than their profits. In most years 20 percent or more of all businesses end the year without a net profit.

Besides its direct financial impact, experience rating has the psychological effect of focusing attention on the prevention of unemployment. Other costs of unemployment, although greater, are more easily overlooked, especially if the responsibility for them is

---

[23] For the explanation of this proposition, see Becker, *Experience Rating*, appendix B.

[24] *Controlling Your Non-Working Payroll Costs: Unemployment Insurance* (New York: Associated Industries of New York State, 1961), p. 27.

[25] Becker, *Experience Rating*, p. 259.

diffused, but the unemployment insurance tax is a distinct cost for which the employer must write a check and is directly traceable to one cause, unemployment. Managers I have interviewed regularly commented on this strategic position of unemployment insurance.[26]

In the Railroad Unemployment Insurance system, contributions are not experience rated. As seen by the individual company in the short run, unemployment benefits are a fixed cost not significantly affected by the extent to which any one company dips into the pooled funds. In their study of employment fluctuations in this industry, William Haber and his coauthors reached the conclusion that the individual railroad companies would be more concerned to avoid unnecessary and violent fluctuations in employment if each had to stand the costs of its own employment policy.[27]

Examples of this sort could be multiplied almost without end,[28] but no lengthening of the list would lead to a reliable estimate of their quantitative importance. Such managerial attempts to lessen unemployment certainly do not constitute anything like a major determinant of the level of unemployment in the economy. Still, some opportunity to lessen frictional and seasonal unemployment seems to pervade a large part of the economy, and it would be incorrect to write off such opportunity as negligible.

The unemployment tax is a minor but constant and sharply focused pressure working throughout the economy, mildly punishing businessmen who become careless or are simply inefficient. The net effect of experience rating on employment stabilization is to be counted a plus. If this were the system's only effect, it would constitute a solid though minor reason for having experience rating.

Business Cycle

This effect is properly considered last because it is the least important of the criteria available by which to evaluate experience rating. The effect is both small and uncertain. Even the total tax is a tiny part (much less than 1 percent) of the economy it is said to influence,

[26] The several examples reported in Becker, *Experience Rating*, pp. 252-58, could easily be multiplied.

[27] William Haber, John J. Carroll, Mark L. Kahn, and Merton J. Peck, *Maintenance of Way Employment on U.S. Railroads* (Detroit, Brotherhood of Maintenance of Way Employees, 1957), pp. 116-26, 228, 230-31.

[28] Two extensive collections of such examples are *The First Wisconsin Conference on Steadier Jobs*, Milwaukee, Wisconsin, June 21, 1940 (Madison: Wisconsin Industrial Commission, 1940), and *To Make Jobs More Steady and to Make More Steady Jobs* (St. Paul: Minnesota American Legion Foundation, 1943).

while the relevant quantity is smaller still, namely, the *difference* between an experience-rated tax and its alternative, a variable uniform tax—that is, a tax that varies in time but is constant for all employers. Even when changes in the total economy are compared with changes in the tax, this ratio remains very small.

The effect is uncertain for several reasons. In the first place, economic science itself is capable neither of predicting cyclical swings nor of fine-tuning the economy to prevent them. When, for example, does the upswing begin? When in the upswing should the tax be raised? By how much? The difficulty would be real enough if a single national tax were involved; it is increased greatly because fifty-one independent state jurisdictions are involved, each differing in its relationship to any national cycle that may be in process. Furthermore, the states differ not only in their economies but in their politics. Many purely political considerations enter into a state's decisions about the size of the fund it wishes to accumulate at any specified time. Even if economic science were able (as it is not) to fine-tune each state's economy, there is no assurance that the game plan prepared by the economist would be followed by the politician.

Whatever small impact experience rating has had on the business cycle seems to have been favorable. A number of statistical studies made during the 1950s and 1960s support that conclusion.[29] These studies provide no basis for the charge that experience rating normally operates to aggravate the business cycle; on the contrary, they indicate that until the 1970s, at least, the experience-rated unemployment insurance tax had operated countercyclically.

This favorable result is not necessarily attributable to experience rating as such. The factors that chiefly accounted for the counter-cyclical impact of the unemployment insurance tax were the brevity of the historial cycles and the timing lag inherent in the tax mechanism. The postwar cycles were relatively short—short enough so that the delayed action of the tax mechanism produced a countercyclical move-ment. By the time the tax began to rise, the recession had run its course, and the economy had begun to recover. In a deeper and more prolonged depression period, the unemployment insurance tax would eventually have a procyclical effect, that is, the tax would begin to rise while the economy was still depressed. Still, this is not a problem of experience rating as such. It is a problem of any system that does not wish to use deficit financing. A uniform, variable tax system would have essentially the same problem if it had to operate in the same political context.

[29] Five of these studies are analyzed in Becker, *Experience Rating*, chap. 11.

Micro Effect. The timing pattern of the experience-rated tax has relevance not only for the business cycle (the macro effect) but also, and more importantly, for the individual firm. During a business cycle not all firms have the same economic experience at the same time. Although the majority of firms are moving in one direction, many others will be moving in the opposite direction. Even the firms that are moving in the same direction will have started at different times and will be moving at different speeds. What is most important in the timing of the tax is that the tax rate of the individual firm fluctuate according to the economic needs of the firm. Without experience rating, changes in the tax over time would have to be on a statewide basis. This would not necessarily fit the needs of individual firms. With experience rating, the timing pattern of the tax can be arranged to fit the pocketbook to which it is most relevant, namely that of the individual firm.

As an example of how the system can work in the case of the individual firm, table 15 shows the financial experience of North American Rockwell Corporation, the California aerospace company whose experience with administration was described earlier in this chapter. At the beginning of fiscal 1960, this company had a reserve (not shown in the table) of $14,398,887. The reserve grew rapidly through 1965, then more slowly through 1968, when it amounted to $48,425,390. This was an amount sufficient to pay benefits for thirteen years at the highest annual rate in its past experience. This healthy balance was to stand the firm in good stead in later years when benefit charges became extremely heavy. As columns seven and eight show, the company grew through 1964 but then experienced a gradual decline that became precipitous toward the end of the period.

In the eleven-year period covered by the table, there were seven years in which the firm's benefit charges increased. The taxes of the firm fell in five of these years, remained practically level in another, and rose in only one. Hence on the whole the tax mechanism acted in a clearly "stabilizing" manner with respect to the firm's own experience. It is worth noting that from 1965 on, the firm's personnel began to shrink, slowly at first and then rapidly, reaching 54 percent of the 1964 size in 1970. Throughout this same period the firm's taxes decreased, dropping from more than $7.0 million to about $1.5 million. This favorable movement of taxes was due primarily to the firm's very large reserves; in these lean years it was truly living off the fat it had stored up in the good years. The tax pattern was due also to the mechanism of the reserve-ratio system, whereby a shrinking payroll

TABLE 15

North American Rockwell Corporation, Aerospace and Systems Group, Unemployment Insurance Tax and Benefit Experience, 1960–1970

Fiscal Year Ending June 30 (1)	Benefit Charges		Taxes[a]		Tax Rate[a,b] (6)	Average Monthly Employment (7)	Taxable Payroll: Change in Year (%) (8)	Reserve Account Balance: Change in Year (%) (9)
	Amount ($ thousands) (2)	Change in year (%) (3)	Amount ($ thousands) (4)	Change in year (%) (5)				
1960	1,032	−25.4	4,017	13.8	2.1	56,474	23.3	20.7
1961	1,195	15.8	3,146	−21.7	1.2	67,630	33.6	11.2
1962	959	−19.8	6,071	92.9	2.1	80,074	15.2	26.4
1963	1,692	76.4	8,513	40.2	2.3	87,949	25.1	27.9
1964	2,360	39.5	8,572	0.7	2.3	89,282	0.7	19.8
1965	3,525	49.4	7,445	−13.2	2.2	85,262	−9.8	10.5
1966	1,689	−52.1	5,466	−26.6	1.6	75,622	1.7	9.1
1967	2,632	55.9	4,108	−24.8	1.3	74,168	−9.6	0.3
1968	2,061	−21.7	3,846	−6.4	1.3	68,314	−4.3	3.8
1969	6,308	206.0	1,493	−61.2	0.6	54,920	−21.7	0.0
1970	10,450	65.7	1,108	−25.8	0.6	47,969	−12.7	−9.9

[a] Excludes balancing tax.
[b] Average tax rate for fiscal year.
SOURCE: Data furnished by firm.

tends to produce a rising reserve ratio and consequently a declining tax rate.

In general, the effect of experience rating on the business cycle is too small and too uncertain to be an important factor in the evaluation of experience rating. If this were the only good effect of experience rating, it would not in itself justify the establishment of experience rating. If this effect were deemed undesirable, it would not outweigh any one of the other good effects. Finally, the flexibility of experience rating enables it to fit the needs of the individual firm that may not be moving with the cycle.

In sum, the list below provides a general view of the terrain traversed in chapters 4 and 5. It enables one to see at a glance the principal answers to be returned to the twin questions that guided the exploration: Are the effects of experience rating large enough to be significant? In their net impact, are these effects desirable? Effects 1, 4, and 5 pertain to the economy and effects 2 and 3 to the unemployment insurance program itself.

Effect on	Significant?	Desirable?
1. Allocation	yes	yes
4. Stabilization	probably	yes
5. Timing	macro: uncertain	yes
	micro: yes	yes
2. Administration	yes	yes
3. Legislation	disqualifications: yes	uncertain
	other: uncertain	uncertain

6

The Taxable Wage Base

Background

In the unemployment insurance financial system, the taxable wage base used by each state must at least equal the base used by the federal government. At the start of the program, Congress set the federal base at total wages. No other base was considered, probably because Congress had not yet perceived the significance of experience rating in the state programs. As early as 1939 Congress changed the federal base to the first $3,000 of wages for a reason that was always of minor importance[1] and allowed the base to remain at that level during the next thirty-two years for the substantive reasons discussed in this chapter. During these years numerous bills were introduced to raise the base, but Congress always—sometimes after intensive hearings—refused to enact them. Congress finally raised the base to $4,200 in 1972 and to $6,000 in 1978. The National Commission on Unemployment Compensation has recommended that the federal base be made a predetermined proportion (eventually reaching 65 percent) of the national annual average of total covered wages.[2]

The states are free to set their base at any level above the federal base, and some states have always chosen to do so. Nevada, which in 1945 was the last state to lower its base to the federal level, was in 1954 the first state to raise its base above the federal level. In succeeding years, other states likewise raised their tax base, a move

[1] The old-age program, popularly known as social security, adopted a taxable wage base of $3,000 for the sound reason that only this amount of wages was used, in the old-age program, to generate benefit rights. The base in unemployment insurance was changed to be the same amount in order to simplify record keeping for employers. In their testimony over the years, employers have consistently reported that this consideration is of little importance.

[2] The national commission has shed little new light on the problem of the taxable wage base. Both its final report and the study paper it commissioned are less adequate treatments of the problem than were in existence before the commission began its work.

usually made on the occasion of a sharp, new need for additional revenue and often accompanied by a simultaneous increase in tax rates. More than twenty states with over half the covered work force had raised their own base before Congress raised the federal base in 1972. The same situation existed before the second raise in 1978. By 1980 sixteen states already had a base higher than the federal requirement of $6,000.

The federal and state bases have not kept up with the great increase in total wages that has occurred since 1940. For a variety of reasons—some sound, some dubious—the ratio of taxable to total wages was allowed to decline gradually to about one-half.[3] It is this long decline in the past, coupled with an expectation of continued inflation of total wages in the future, that has made the taxable wage base a pressing issue in the present.

The determination of the tax base is the most difficult and least satisfactory task in the financing of unemployment insurance. Given the present structure of the program, a logically satisfactory solution to the problem is probably out of reach. We can, however, identify the major parts of the problem and analyze their interrelationships. Although this exercise will not necessarily tell us what a tax base ought to be, it can help develop guiding principles.

There are four elements, or groups of elements, that must be fitted together in the final solution. Briefly, they are (1) two roads to two objectives, (2) two norms of equity, (3) two taxes, and (4) multiple state situations.

Two Roads to Two Objectives

In financing unemployment insurance, it is necessary to attain two objectives, adequacy and equity. That is, the amount of taxes must be adequate to meet the program's obligations, and the distribution of the tax burden must be equitable.[4] To this twofold objective there is

---

[3] See table 3, where the average state ratio of taxable to total wages is shown by year, 1957-1978.

[4] The relationship of the tax mechanism to the business cycle is also a consideration. The closer the taxable wage base comes to total wages, the more likely it is that the tax system will work countercyclically. This effect is, however, never certain—depending as it does on a variety of changing and unpredictable factors—and is never major. Among the considerations that dictate the choice of a tax base, this possible effect ranks near the bottom of the list. For what it is worth, it may be noted that the actual tax has a good historical record of countercyclical movement; see Joseph M. Becker, *Experience Rating in Unemployment Insurance* (Baltimore: Johns Hopkins University Press, 1972), chap. 11.

a twofold road, tax base and tax rate. These, like the two blades of a scissors, determine both adequacy and equity. Within certain limits, not clearly definable, there is an almost infinite variety of possible base/rate combinations. Logically, it is impossible to settle on a tax base without at the same time taking cognizance of actual and intended tax rates.

In selecting a base, one must accord the objective of adequacy a certain practical primacy in the sense that adequacy limits smallness. A tax rate of even 100 percent will not raise sufficient revenue if the tax base is only $1.00. Adequacy, however, is a straightforward issue of no great theoretical complexity. The more difficult issue—and the central concern of this chapter (as indeed of the whole book)—is equity. The chapter is focused on the way the tax base affects equity in the unemployment insurance financing structure—always remembering that the four elements of adequacy and equity and base and rate are in fact inextricably intertwined.

Two Norms of Equity

How does the selection of a tax base affect the distribution of the tax burden, and what is the most equitable distribution? The answer depends largely on the selection of norms of equity. The principal norms governing the equitable distribution of unemployment insurance taxes are the usual two: benefit received and ability to pay.[5] The relative weight assigned to each norm will depend on the tax situation to which they are applied. For example, the fee charged by a government for use of a bridge is governed chiefly by the benefit-received norm, whereas the progressive character of the income tax is governed chiefly by the ability-to-pay norm. Insofar as unemployment insurance is a social *insurance* program, it will be governed by benefit received, but insofar as it is a *social* insurance program it will also be governed by ability to pay.

The extent to which one accords the preeminence to one or the other of these norms chiefly accounts for the way one judges equity in unemployment insurance financing. Much, probably most, of the dispute over the "right" tax base is traceable to the different weights the disputants assign to these two norms. If disputants first of all made clear to each other where they stand on the prior and more fundamental issue, their subsequent debate would be more fruitful.

---

[5] The norm of equality of sacrifice is less a separate norm than another form, the obverse, of ability to pay. This may be seen in the ordering of norms in, for example, Harold M. Groves, *Financing Government* (New York: Henry Holt & Co., 1939), chap. 2.

Historically, the financing of unemployment insurance has been governed primarily by the benefit-received norm. This accounts for the settling of financial responsibility on the individual state, on the individual employer, and on the employer in some proportion to his use of the program. Unemployment insurance has been made a regular cost of doing business; as a result its benefits are properly considered to be, not welfare, but an extension of the wage system. The wage system is governed primarily by the benefit-received norm. Nevertheless, the attempt is sometimes made to apply ability to pay to unemployment insurance and in two ways. First, the norm is given an analogous meaning, but thus understood, it is applied validly. Second, the norm is expressed univocally, but thus understood, it is applied invalidly.

In its first and analogously valid application, the norm has a purely economic and political significance. It does not have the moral connotation that it does, for example, in the progressive income tax. Firms are subsidized in unemployment insurance not for the sake of the individual firm but for the sake of the general economy or because political forces in the state so dictate. The apparel industry of New York furnishes a good example. The employers in this industry have been accorded a special (low) maximum rate because they have been going out of business or moving to other parts of the country. Wanting to retain the industry for New York, the state legislators, especially those whose constituents are dependent on the industry, seek to lighten the industry's financial burdens, even if only in a minor way. Hence all other employers are required to furnish a subsidy to employers in the apparel industry. The usual political dynamics are at work here: Because the subsidy is more concentrated in its payees than in its payers, opposition to the subsidy is weaker than the demand for it.

When the American Retail Federation stated its policy regarding unemployment insurance in 1980, it recognized that to some extent financial logic would have to yield to political pressures in the selection of a taxable wage base. "This is the most controversial issue among employers, as it tends to pit high-wage and steady employers [those paying high annual wages] against low-wage employers and employers having large numbers of part-time or seasonal employees [those paying low annual wages]. Therefore, establishing a wage base above the minimum usually requires a compromise."[6]

---

[6] *Unemployment Compensation Retail Objectives Technical Material* (Washington, D.C.: Retailers Task Force on State Unemployment Compensation by American Retail Federation, 1980), p. B-8.

This political understanding of "ability to pay" explains an illogical characteristic of the tax structure in the states that utilize alternative tax schedules. In the lower tax schedules, used when the fund is full, *all* the rates may be lower, including the maximum rate. But the employers at the maximum rate are usually deficit employers, who ought to be paying more if they can. If they can pay more when the fund is low, usually in worse times, they should be able to pay more in good times. Only politics explains why the *maximum* rate is lowered in good times.

'Effective' Rate. Ability to pay in its other meaning is of dubious validity and perhaps for that reason has had little effect on the program. It is, however, the argument on which the proponents of a high tax base mainly rely. It is based on the distinction between high-wage and low-wage firms.[7] If, for example, A is a high-wage and B a low-wage employer and both pay the same tax, the tax represents a higher proportion of total wages for B than for A. The users of this argument term this unequal proportion inequitable. How the transition is effected from unequal to inequitable is not explained by any of the argument's users, but the argument would seem to rest on three assumptions: (1) the high-wage firm is the more profitable firm and therefore has the greater ability to pay; (2) the norm of ability to pay, understood in this moral sense, applies to business costs; (3) total wages are encompassed by the unemployment insurance program.

Instead of attempting to establish these assumptions, the users of the argument rely simply on the expression "effective tax rate." Whereas they call the tax in relation to taxable wages the nominal rate, they call the tax in relation to total wages the effective rate. The implication is that taxes in proportion to total wages is the "real" rate in some sense that is left unexplained and unproved.

The first assumption has a prima facie plausibility. If a firm can afford to pay high wages, it probably can afford to pay high taxes. Still, that assumption is open to several qualifications. A firm's ability

[7] It appears in Eugene C. McKean, *The Taxable Wage Base in Unemployment Insurance Financing* (Kalamazoo, Mich.: W. E. Upjohn Institute for Employment Research, 1965), chap. 3; in William Haber and Merrill G. Murray, *Unemployment Insurance in the American Economy* (Homewood, Ill.: Richard D. Irwin, 1966), chap. 18; and in National Commission on Unemployment Compensation, *Unemployment Compensation: Final Report* (Washington, D.C., July 1980), pp. 80-86. Throughout the discussion of "effective" tax rates, high and low wages must be understood as *annual* wages. Annual wages paid to a given employee by a given employer are determined not only by wage rates but also by continuity of employment.

to meet a labor cost is dependent on many factors—for example, whether it is labor intensive or capital intensive—but chiefly on its profitability. Some low-wage firms are enormously profitable, whereas some high-wage firms are in danger of bankruptcy. None of the argument's users have made any effort to measure the correlation, if any, between levels of wages and levels of profits. Without such a measured correlation, the argument hangs in the thin air of conjecture and provides no reliable basis for policy.

The second assumption is even more vulnerable to criticism. In the United States, unemployment insurance is a regular cost of doing business, and business costs are not normally adjusted to a firm's ability to pay. An employer pays his own costs, whatever they are, or he goes out of business. If he is granted a cost concession, it is for some reason other than the welfare of the individual firm—either to help the economy of the state or for strictly political reasons. Business taxes are not governed by the same principles that apply to the personal income tax.

Examination of the third assumption further undermines the validity of the effective-tax argument. In a program like unemployment insurance, where the tax has been made a regular business cost, the only wages that have significance for the tax base are those used for the benefit base. The remainder of total wages, since they are not used to establish benefit rights, are outside the unemployment insurance program and are properly ignored. Unemployment insurance is by its nature and design a limited program. A limited proportion of the work force is eligible for a limited proportion of its wages for a limited period. It is only within these limits that quantities matter. Workers and wages outside these limits are of no concern to the unemployment insurance program as it has legally been established and is currently functioning. The program could of course be altered, but that is another matter altogether. The actual unemployment insurance program is concerned with only a limited proportion of wages, that used for benefits and taxes.

The effective-tax argument has a cousin, another argument based on a term. A tax on anything less than total wages is called regressive. Technically, a regressive tax decreases in rate as income and ability to pay increase. The notion of regressivity is applicable strictly to an income tax and in a somewhat extended sense to a sales tax. Normally it does not apply to a business tax.

Perhaps the argument assumes that the tax (a small part? all of it?) is ultimately paid not by the employer or consumer but by the employee. Still, this assumption encounters two difficulties. In the first place it is next to impossible to follow the shifting and final

116

incidence of any small payroll tax, a difficulty that is trebled when the tax is experience rated. The high degree of uncertainty thus attaching to the argument makes it useless as a base for practical policy. Further, no matter who ultimately pays the tax—employer, consumer, or employee—it remains, like other payroll costs, a part of the competitive market rather than of the welfare system and hence governed not by the norm of ability to pay but by the norm of benefit received.

Two Taxes

Unemployment insurance is supported by two separate though interdependent taxes. One is a relatively small, uniform, federal tax used primarily to pay administrative costs, including those of the states. It has also been used to build a loan fund and in recent years to pay the federal part of extended benefits. The other is a state tax that is much larger, variable, usually experience rated, and used only to pay benefits.[8]

As mentioned earlier, Congress has raised the federal tax base only twice but has manipulated the federal tax rate more frequently. Changes in the federal base have affected the states much more than changes in the federal rate. The state base must, in effect, be at least as high as the federal base, and most states have had to raise their base when the federal base rose. In changing the rate, however, Congress has thus far always stipulated that the maximum standard rate would remain 2.7 percent (90 percent of 3 percent). In 1980, the federal tax was 3.4 percent, but with the 2.7 percent offset remaining unchanged, the actual federal tax was thus 0.7 percent (on $6,000). In 1980, sixteen states had tax bases in excess of the required $6,000, and practically all of the states had maximum tax rates in excess of the required 2.7 percent. The states do have a substantial history of going beyond federal requirements as they have seen the need to do so.

Two conclusions may be drawn from this brief description of the two taxes. First, as long as the present law prevails, a change in the federal tax base will usually have a substantial effect on state tax structures, but a change in the federal tax rate will probably have no

---

[8] The actual tax structure is more complex than this simple description suggests. A full federal tax is levied that is large enough to support the payment of all benefits, but this full tax is not actually paid, nor can it be used to pay benefits. The employer may offset 90 percent of the federal tax by the payment of a similar tax to the state government. He may claim this offset even though his payment to the state is less than the full 90 percent allowed—*if* the reduced state tax is attributable to the employer's favorable "experience" with unemployment.

effect at all. From the viewpoint of state freedom and flexibility, therefore, a change in the federal rate is preferable to a change in the federal base. This consideration, as a matter of fact, chiefly influenced Congress to change the rate rather than the base on the half-dozen occasions when it needed to increase the flow of federal revenues.

Second, because the federal and state taxes are so different in both objective and operation, it would be best to disconnect their bases. This would go far toward making possible a logically satisfactory solution of the tax base problem. The federal government would be free to set its base to meet its own needs without having to consider how its action would affect the states.

Congress could disconnect the two bases in a number of ways. The simplest way might be for Congress to handle future changes in the tax base in the same way that it has handled changes in the tax rate in the past, namely, without requiring the states to match the full federal tax change. For example, whatever the federal base, Congress could continue the allowance of full credit against the $4,200 base for state offset purposes. This would give the states the same kind of freedom over their tax base that they have had over their tax rate. Congress would retain adequate control over the system by means of the two limited offsets, the 2.7 percent rate and the $4,200 base. Indeed, even if the offset device were abandoned entirely, Congress could maintain adequate control by its power over the administrative funds.

Federal Tax. The main part of this tax is used for administration. On the reasonable assumption that the cost of serving high-wage and low-wage employers is about the same, the benefit-received norm would dictate something like a poll tax, a flat amount for each employee covered.[9] The federal tax more closely approximates a poll tax when the tax base is kept low.

The part of the federal tax used for other than administrative purposes raises an additional issue. The employees of high-wage employers may draw more from the federal fund than do the employees of low-wage employers. (This is true not because high-wage employers have more unemployment but because their employees are eligible for higher benefits.) To the extent that this is so, it furnishes a reason for setting the federal base somewhat higher than the admin-

[9] Theoretically, the correspondence between tax and benefit received could be made closer by taking cognizance of the effect on administrative expenses of such factors as state variations in salaries, cost of living, and concentration of population, but these niceties are not the stuff of workable policies.

istrative function alone would make appropriate.

The issue of equity as applied to the federal tax must remain ambiguous as long as the tax is used for different objectives. One solution would be to use the federal tax solely for administration. The loan fund could easily, since it is a revolving fund, be financed from general revenues. All, and not just half, of the cost of extended benefits could be borne by each state.[10] With the federal tax thus unambiguously related to administrative costs, it would be easy to conclude that the base of the tax should be set as low as possible, so as (1) to resemble a poll tax as closely as possible and (2) to leave each state maximum freedom in selecting its own tax base.

It is probably desirable to index the federal base, that is, to link it automatically to the national average wage. Indexing has two advantages. First, it ensures against the likelihood that Congress, busy with its multitudinous duties, will overlook the need for timely adjustment of the wage base. Given the near certainty of continually rising wages, an automatic adjustment of the taxable portion of wages would provide an element of stability, of predictability.

The second advantage stems precisely from this enhanced predictability. A predetermined federal base would remove any expectation by some states that Congress was about to act to change the base. A state might fear such congressional action and postpone its own action, lest it have to adjust its tax structure twice in rapid succession. More often, a state might hope for congressional action as a way of escaping the blame for raising taxes—the blame can be placed on "the Feds." [11] Still, again the result is to postpone state action.

The passivity of the states in waiting for federal leadership that the national commission noted is closely connected with such expectations. If the states had known for certain over the life of the program that they could not look to Congress to determine the state base, more of them would certainly have acted on their own initiative. This is the general opinion of those observers intimately connected with the program.

---

[10] "Extended benefits" here are understood to include only the extension to thirty-nine weeks. Beyond that lies the system of federal supplemental benefits, which, as the name suggests, are properly financed out of general revenues.

[11] In 1975 the Unemployment Insurance Committee of ICESA recommended an indexed federal base obligatory for the states. When I asked the chairman of the committee why ICESA preferred federal over state action in raising the base, he replied: "The reason for federal action rather than state action was that most of us [state administrators] felt it would be hard to pass an increase in tax base through our own legislative bodies. A federal requirement would be simpler and more expeditious" (letter to author dated February 12, 1981). In 1980 the Board of Directors of ICESA reaffirmed this recommendation.

State Tax. As argued above, equity in the state tax is governed primarily by the benefit-received norm. If the state tax were perfectly experience rated, so that every employer was self-supporting over the long run, the question of how the base is related to equity would probably never be raised. Any combination of tax base and rate that produced perfect "benefit" equity would be acceptable. It would make no significant difference to an employer whether the state extracted X number of dollars from him by means of a high rate on a low base or by a low rate on a high base. The number of dollars owed would be the same, determined solely by each employer's own experience. Perfect experience rating is, of course, out of reach, but the closer it is approached, the less the tax base matters in relation to tax equity. The first and most telling action a state could take to solve the puzzle of equity in relation to the tax base would be to increase the maximum tax rate.

Since, in fact, some employers are subsidized and others are subsidizers, a situation foreseen and intended, the selection of a base does become an issue of equity. The legislator must inquire how an increase in the base will affect the size of the subsidy and the distribution of the burden (of providing the subsidy) among taxpayers. The calculation of these two effects is complex and uncertain. The following is a simplified example of the kind of investigation involved.

The example [12] shows how, under given assumptions, an increase in the wage base will affect six different classes of firms. The six classes are derived from cross-classifying two levels of wages by three levels of benefit cost. The three levels of benefit cost are represented by three tax rates. In the reserve-ratio system, which is used by most states, firms pay the maximum rate, the minimum rate, or the "natural" rate. The natural rate is the equilibrium rate toward which all firms tend and at which a firm's tax rate equals its benefit-cost rate.

Table 16 shows the total additional taxes that the six classes of firms in Michigan would have paid over a fifteen-year period (1958–1972) if the base in Michigan had been raised from $3,000 to $4,800. All firms in the example have the same number of employees (500). The hourly rate in the high-wage firms is assumed to be $3.00 and in the low-wage firms $1.80. The maximum tax rate during the period is assumed to be 4.0 percent; the minimum rate, 0.5 percent. The firms at the maximum tax rate are assumed to have 162 workers unemployed for thirteen weeks each year; the firms at the natural rate

[12] The example is compiled from data provided by McKeon, *Taxable Wage Base*, pp. 64ff. McKean's 1965 analysis of the tax base is still the best treatment of the subject.

TABLE 16

ADDITIONAL TAXES DUE FROM MICHIGAN FIRMS FOR A FIFTEEN-YEAR PERIOD FOLLOWING A TAX-BASE INCREASE FROM $3,000 TO $4,800

Type of Firm	Additional Taxes (dollars)	
Maximum rate		
High wage	366,500	—
Low wage	—	130,800
Natural rate		
High wage	84,600	—
Low wage	—	25,500
Minimum rate		
High wage	133,700	—
Low wage	—	52,600
All high wage	584,800	—
All low wage	—	208,900
All maximum rate	497,300	—
All others	—	296,400

SOURCE: See footnote 12.

have 108 workers unemployed for thirteen weeks each year; the firms at the minimum rate have no workers unemployed each year.

The three high-wage firms contributed more than twice as much as the three low-wage firms: $584,800 as against $208,900. Some such shifting of the burden onto high-wage firms will normally result from raising the wage base. This result is an important political factor, one likely to influence a state's decision independently of any other results.

There are other results. The effect on "benefit" equity is shown in the final pair of groupings. The firms at the maximum tax rate, most of which are probably deficit operations, contributed $497,300, whereas all the remaining firms contributed a total of $296,400.[13]

[13] The explanation of this difference lies in the mechanism of the reserve-ratio system. In brief, the additional taxes paid by the self-supporting firms build up their reserves and eventually lower their tax rates to a point where their dollar taxes are the same as before the base was changed. Still, many of the deficit firms remain deficit, and their tax rate, the maximum, remains the same. They continue, therefore, to pay higher dollar taxes indefinitely. (A different analysis, with different effects, would apply in a state with an experience-rating system other than reserve ratio.)

Any additional contribution made by deficit firms is a move toward greater equity as measured by benefit received. On the other hand, any additional contribution by self-supporting and subsidizing firms is a move away from such equity. Since the deficit firms contributed almost twice as much as the other firms, the net effect of the enlarged tax base may be described as a gain in equity as measured by benefit received.

To end the analysis at this point would be to leave the reasoning essentially incomplete. A decision on the wage base cannot be made logically apart from consideration of the alternative, an increase in the tax rate. If some or all of the total additional $793,700 had been attained by raising the maximum tax rate instead of enlarging the base, the increase in equity as measured by benefit received would have been greater. This will always be true. Under any and all assumptions, the use of the rate as compared with the use of the base will increase equity as measured by benefit received.

One of the arguments enlisted in favor of an enlarged tax base is that such action is needed to increase the degree of experience rating (equity as measured by benefit received) in the system. In light of the analysis above, this proposition must be distinguished. If we compare enlarging the base with doing nothing, then to enlarge the base is to increase the degree of experience rating. If we compare enlarging the base with raising the maximum tax rate, however, then the stated objective (improvement of experience rating) can be better attained by raising the rate than by enlarging the base. Ultimately, the reason is that an increase in the maximum tax rate affects all and only deficit firms, whereas an enlargement of the tax base affects deficit and self-supporting firms alike.

The example above illustrates one of many possible situations. Different assumptions will produce different results.[14] Different possible assumptions include the following: a different average total wage for the state; a different definition of high- and low-wage firms; a different mix of such firms, however defined; different maximum and minimum rates and different schedules to produce the natural rate; a different length of time over which the various effects are measured; different levels of unemployment within the period over which the effects are measured; an experience-rating system other than reserve ratio. Although not complete, the list is long enough to

[14] Charles B. Little, of the *Unemployment Benefit Advisor*, provided many other examples in a presentation to the NCUC in September 1978. Little's general conclusion was: "The tables show that an increase in the taxable wage base hits hardest those employers that have the lower benefit cost rates, regardless of whether they are low-wage or high-wage employers" (unpublished ms., p. 12).

indicate the problem of predicting how an increase in the federal wage base will affect equity in each of the states needing to match the federal increase. If the federal base had been raised in 1980, about two-thirds of the states would have had to raise their bases. It is impossible to predict how equity among taxpayers would be affected in each of these states.

It is useful to note that several studies have found no correlation between industry levels of wages and industry levels of cost. This was the conclusion reached, for example, in a 1964 study by New York and in a 1967 study by California. To quote California: "It is just as inaccurate to say that high-wage industries are high-cost industries as it is to say that they are low-cost industries."[15]

Given the great variation among the states—with respect to wage, tax, and benefit systems—it is not to be expected that one solution of the tax base problem will fit all states. Still, in selecting its taxable wage base, a state would do well to start with the principle that those wages used as the base for benefits should also be used as the base for taxes. This principle makes for a logical tax structure. It will not, however, be universally applicable. For example, as of 1980, this principle would have required West Virginia to have a taxable wage base of $15,000 and New York a base of less than $5,000. Neither state is likely to see these bases as practicable. Nevertheless, this principle is the best starting place, to be applied as far as possible. To the extent that the principle cannot be applied, a state might ask itself whether there is something awry with its benefit formula. A state may be requiring too much or too little in the way of earnings in order to qualify for its maximum benefit. In general, however, a state should make certain that it includes in the tax base all wages that are used to establish benefits. As of January 1980, thirty-nine states used more wages for benefits than they used for taxes.

Multiple State Differences

An increase in the federal tax base has two effects. Besides its direct effect on federal revenues, it has an indirect effect on the tax structures of the states, all of which are required (in practice) to have a base at least as high as the federal. The second effect is by far the more important.

The effect on the states will vary by state according to a long list of differences, such as size, industrial and occupational character-

---

[15] Unpublished working paper, actuarial division, California Employment Development Department, p. 6.

istics, average wage, kind of unemployment insurance program (especially kind of experience-rating system), condition of the unemployment insurance fund, and patterns of economic growth or decline. States also differ in their values. Two states might experience about the same economic effect from a rise in the tax base and yet evaluate that effect differently. The overwhelming impression one receives from working with the states is that of heterogeneity. A base equal to 65 percent of the *national* average wage (the commission's recommendation) has a significance for Michigan that differs from that for Mississippi. (The national commission's use of the effective tax argument invites the observation that the commission wishes to impose a higher "effective" tax base on Mississippi than on Michigan.)

The heterogeneity of the states also has a historical dimension. The current program in each state reflects past bargains struck over the years between various interest groups and incorporated into the state's political fabric. When the federal government raises the federal tax base, it imposes on the states a requirement unadjusted to state differences and innocent of state history.

The NCUC is ambivalent regarding this imposition. On the one hand it clearly intends Congress to impose a uniform requirement on the states. It judges that the states have been deficient and need to be forced to action "because so many states are passive in adjusting their bases and await action by the Congress."[16] On the other hand, the commission seems to argue that Congress would not really be imposing its preference on the states, because the states can, if they desire, "offset the impact of an increase in the base by adjusting the tax rate schedule."[17] On balance, it is clear that the commission wishes Congress to require most states to do what they prefer not to do. Of any state that prefers a low base/high rate combination the commission demands a high base/low rate combination.

Why have the states allowed the taxable/total wage ratio to decline? The reasons are multiple and differ from state to state, but three apply rather generally. First, the extraordinarily large reserves accumulated during the war had the effect of discouraging any move that would increase revenues (see chapter 2). Second, the states have had a preference for the benefit-received norm and have chosen to raise rates when they did need additional revenue. Practically all states have raised their maximum rate beyond the federal requirement. Third, the states expected, and some chose to await, congressional

16 *Unemployment Compensation: Final Report*, p. 81.
17 Ibid., p. 84.

124

action on one or another of the many bills introduced during the past few years to raise the federal base. Their two reasons for waiting were mentioned above.

There have always been a substantial number of states, usually more than twenty, that have raised their bases beyond the federal requirement on their own initiative as they saw the need. In all probability, states will continue to act on their own initiative as they see the need. By 1980 sixteen states had already moved beyond the federal base of $6,000 established in 1978.

Guidelines

The preceding analysis provides the basis for sketching a few guidelines for policy, some of them general, others pertaining specifically to the federal or the state taxes.

General. Among the general guidelines, three are especially useful.

1. *Recognize that the norm of benefit received is the primary measure of equity in unemployment insurance.* In practice, this means a preferential reliance on the tax rate rather than on the tax base.[18]

Understood in its strict sense, the ability-to-pay norm is not applicable to unemployment insurance, a business cost. Understood, however, in the analogous sense described in the text—and for the two reasons given there—it is sometimes applicable.

2. *Disconnect the state base from the federal base.* This would be the single biggest step toward making possible a logically satisfactory solution of the tax base problem. Freeing the state from the federal base would not deprive the federal government of needed control over the states.

3. *Abandon the argument derived from the notion of an "effective" tax rate.* This argument depends on three assumptions, of which one is unproved and the other two are erroneous. Its continued use will continue to mislead.

Federal Tax Base. Only two guidelines suggest themselves as useful specifically for the federal base.

1. *Keep the federal base as low as possible.* This principle stems from two considerations. First, insofar as federal revenues are

---

[18] At hearings held by the National Commission on Unemployment Compensation in Washington, D.C., July 1978, a representative of the National Association of Manufacturers during the questioning period said: "Most of my clients are small firms with low wages. Nevertheless I favor a smaller tax base and a greater range of tax rates rather than the opposite alternative."

used principally for administrative costs, something like a poll tax is appropriate. The federal tax will approach a poll tax more closely when the base of the tax is kept low. Second, as long as the state and federal taxes are interconnected, a lower federal base will allow the states greater freedom and flexibility. Contrariwise, the higher the federal base, the more confining is the straitjacket imposed on the (very heterogeneous) states.[19]

2. *Index for federal tax base.* A self-adjusted base, set as a proportion of the national average wage, would (a) guard against congressional neglect and (b) lessen the temptation of states to use federal unpredictability as an excuse for their own inaction.

In the light of general guideline 1, the indexed base should be kept relatively low, perhaps set at 40–50 percent of the national average wage. Irregular variations in revenue needs could be met by adjustments in the tax rate.[20]

State Tax Base. If the federal base is disconnected from the state base, or is kept low if left connected, each state will be free to choose its own tax base. Given the great heterogeneity of state circumstances, varying not only between states but also over time, only a few general guidelines for state action can be identified.

1. *Adopt a schedule for tax rates that will produce the desired degree of experience rating.*[21] Following general guideline 1, a state should start with the rate structure, rather than with the base, and establish a maximum tax rate as high as the state economy, and politics, will permit. With respect to the limitation imposed by the state economy, many states would be well advised to experiment with a higher maximum rate. A higher maximum may be imposed more safely the more gradually it is approached. A declared policy of small annual increments may eventually produce a maximum significantly higher than had at first been thought possible. (Employers are accustomed to paying the much higher maximum rates in the state programs of workmen's compensation.) The eventual goal might be a stated percentage of employers at the maximum rate. If this percentage begins to grow, the maximum rate should be increased.

[19] The preference of the NCUC for an increase in the base rather than in the rate has two roots: (a) acceptance of the argument for an effective tax as a measure of equity and (b) desire to force the states to raise their bases.

[20] In the past, whenever Congress has raised the federal tax rate, it has left unchanged the 2.7 percent offset, thus leaving undiminished the states' freedom to set their own maximum rate. Those who favor congressional action that would force states to raise their maximum tax rate, while opposing similar action regarding the tax base, are not consistent.

[21] See tables 12 and 13 for examples of measuring degrees of experience rating.

A state should always have a minimum rate of zero. Unplanned distortions inevitably enter the tax system with a minimum rate above zero. The necessary pooled costs are better financed by a special social tax levied on all employers, such as those now levied by a dozen states, than by a minimum above zero.

2. *Tax only, and preferably all, wages used to establish benefit entitlement.* This is not an absolute principle, because in a few states it would dictate a base out of proportion to benefits actually paid. For most states, however, this is a logical and useful guideline. Coupled with a tax schedule already selected, the tax base thus chosen may produce excess or deficient revenues. If there are excess revenues, the base should be narrrowed; if revenues are deficient, the base should be enlarged. The closer the rate schedule comes to perfect experience rating, the less it will matter, from the viewpoint of tax equity, what the base is. The principal consideration in the selection of a base will then be tax adequacy. The application of the benefit-received norm is limited chiefly by the simple fact that most of the wages of the system are in the low-cost firms, which have to be taxed above their costs in order to obtain the money needed to run the system.

3. *Index the state tax base.* This is the least certain of the guidelines. A state legislature will find it easier to monitor its own base and make needed changes from time to time than Congress would for all the states simultaneously. Hence there may not be the same need for state as for federal indexing. Moreover, a base set automatically would lessen the freedom of a state legislature to reach a given end by adjusting the rate rather than the base, as the legislature might prefer to do.

Nevertheless, an indexed base has advantages, especially for stability. Once a satisfactory rate/base combination has been established, it should be maintained, other things being equal. The tax specialists have a saying, "An old tax is a good tax," meaning that the economy has had a chance to adjust to an old tax. Although an indexed base is by definition a changing quantity, what matters chiefly is not the absolute amount of the base but its relationships (to wages, benefits, and tax rates). True, an indexed base will draw additional taxes from low-cost employers, but since all employers' potential liabilities are increasing along with wages, all employers should probably be building up larger reserves. The impact on low-cost employers will be controlled if the minimum tax rate is zero.

In principle, it would be desirable to link the index with three variables: changes in total wages, condition of the reserve fund, and changes in the amount of wages used for benefits. Practically, the index would probably have to be linked only with changes in total wages. Thirteen states[22] have already adopted such a base, but their short experience has not yet been analyzed—not even by the NCUC—for the lessons it may have to teach.

The major guidelines might be summed up thus. The federal base should be disconnected from the state base. Whether or not this is done, the federal base should be kept as low as possible and probably should be indexed. In selecting its tax base, a state should be guided by two complementary considerations: As far as possible, it should tax those wages that are used for benefits; it should achieve a base/rate combination that will produce the desired degree of experience rating. A base thus selected should be modified only as it produces excess or deficient revenues. It is less necessary, but probably desirable, to index the state base.

---

[22] Alaska, Hawaii, Idaho, Iowa, Montana, Nevada, New Jersey, New Mexico, North Dakota, Oregon, Rhode Island, Utah, and Washington. All but three of these (Oregon, Utah, and Washington) use the reserve-ratio system of experience rating. The impact of a change in the wage base is much greater in the reserve-ratio system than in the other systems.

7
Review and Prescription

This study has evaluated two of the original decisions made in the financing of unemployment insurance, the decisions to make each state and each firm responsible for their own costs. The appraisal drew on the distinction between "individualistic" and "socialistic" approaches to the solution of social problems. As they are used here, both terms refer not to a concrete political structure but merely to a characteristic approach—a general tendency to solve problems by reliance on individual responsibility or on social responsibility.

The Jefferson-Hamilton debate, mentioned in the beginning of chapter 2, has become more complex with the passage of time, mirroring the growth in complexity of a technological society as well as the growth of interest groups so powerful as to require a powerful controlling government. It is even less possible now than it was earlier to make a simple, undifferentiated choice between the pure forms of the two values. The choice requires a delicate balancing of both—the kind of balance, I should say, that is reflected in the unemployment insurance system. Indeed, I doubt that there is any better example of an imaginative blending of both values than unemployment insurance.

The choice between the individualistic and socialistic approaches had to be made repeatedly in the series of decisions that brought unemployment insurance into existence in the United States. We first had to decide whether to have compulsory unemployment insurance at all. Such a program represents a socialistic intervention in the individualistic market. We made the socialistic choice in 1935. Next we had to decide whether to locate financial responsibility in the national government or to require each state to be responsible for its own program. We made the more individualistic choice of separate state programs. We had also to decide on the kind of tax to be levied in support of the program. The more general the tax, the more socialistic are its effects. For the most part, we have chosen the most narrowly focused of all possible taxes, a payroll tax payable only by employers subject to the law.

Next we had to decide whether to tax all employers at a uniform rate or to vary the rate with individual employer experience. Although we have generally made the more individualistic choice of experience rating, we have stopped short of complete experience rating and have provided for a significant degree of sharing of unemployment benefit costs. In what might be termed characteristic American fashion, after grafting some individualistic, competitive branches on to the socialistic vine of unemployment insurance, we proceeded to graft some socialistic twigs onto the branches.

It is this hybrid of competitive socialism that has been under review. In the light of forty-five years of experience, what judgment is to be rendered on the wisdom or folly of the original choices: Has experience proved clearly that the competitive emphasis was a mistake and that a more socialistic approach would have been better? If so, the burden of proof imposed by the vertical lines of figure 1 would have been met and the way cleared for a decision to change the system in the future.

Yet the answer to that question is certainly "no." Such clear evidence does not exist. Since the competitive approach begins with a preferred position and enjoys the benefit of the doubt, a lack of evidence would—at the very least—leave the original choice still in possession of the field. Still, there is actually more to be said: The evidence indicates that the original choices worked out well and probably better than the alternatives would have.

State Responsibility

By the first criterion of any financing system, the states performed responsibly: They paid all claims. Funds were always available to pay the covenanted benefits. On occasion some states needed to borrow funds, an action to be evaluated in the light of the context developed in chapter 2. In the first forty years of the program's operation, only three states borrowed, of which only two actually used the loan. The 1974–1975 recession marked the first serious dependence on the loan fund. This was an extraordinary development, explainable in terms of exceptional circumstances that are not likely to be, and certainly need not be, repeated.

All state debts have been or will be repaid. As long as this essential condition is maintained, the fact of borrowing does not of itself indicate fiscal irresponsibility. Borrowing followed by repayment is an accepted and common business procedure. There has been no serious support for proposals to cancel any of the state debts. (I am speaking here, as always, of the regular program; the program of federal supplemental benefits is another matter altogether, requiring a different and separate kind of financial machinery.) One of the most striking aspects of the hearings conducted by the NCUC was the unbroken testimony of employers that they were prepared to pay off the debts of their respective states and did not want federal assistance. This was the position of employers even in such states as Illinois and Pennsylvania, with their massive debts. There is every indication that the states, without exception, will live up to their responsibility.

A National Program. Granted that the performance of the states has been reasonably good, might not the system have turned in a still better performance using a more socialistic approach? In this context, "better" is taken to mean "more liberal." The assumption that more is always better is obviously open to question. There must be some limit to liberality, at which point the more liberal is not the better. Still, if we grant the assumption, the interesting question may be asked: Why did the states not do "better"? Presumably the reason was that they were either unwilling or unable.

If they were unwilling, the remedy is to be found in federal standards or in a completely nationalized program. I have discussed the option of federal standards elsewhere.[1] Since we have never had a single national program, a discussion of this option must proceed by conjecture, with a considerable element of personal opinion.

I am inclined to believe that a national program would not have been more liberal than the one we have and might very well have been less liberal. Such a program would have been formed by the average of influences at work in the national Congress. Some indication of what that average would have produced may be found in the way the Congress has regularly responded to one major effort to liberalize the program, the effort to enact federal benefit standards. Since the beginning of the system, bills to enact federal benefit standards have repeatedly been introduced in Congress and have as repeatedly been rejected. Since the less liberal states have always been in the majority, this result is understandable. These same states would have been in the majority in any legislation to determine the provisions of a national system. I am inclined to judge that in a national program a level of liberality would have been struck somewhat higher than that of the least liberal states but somewhat lower than that of the most liberal states. This national level would have represented a degree of liberality *per worker* lower than that achieved in the actual program

[1] Joseph M. Becker, *Unemployment Benefits: Should There Be a Compulsory Federal Standard?* (Washington, D.C.: American Enterprise Institute, 1980).

because most covered workers have lived in the more liberal states.

The most notable advances in liberality have been in the areas of coverage and benefit duration. In both these areas the individual states have moved long before the Congress moved. The typical pattern has been for a few states to move out in front and then, after a sufficient number of other states have followed their example, for Congress to move. The *threat* of congressional action has been a separate factor but has usually become a significant force only after individual states have already moved.

Individual states have adopted such innovative provisions as the flexible maximum benefit and the flexible wage base. The future will probably resemble the past and will probably see a continuous, if gradual, adoption by states of provisions and techniques that have proved their worth in the experience of other states. Pioneering, innovative states never seem to be lacking. The present system allows individual states to move out ahead of the pack. They are not tied to the entire mass of the system. As some states do adopt more liberal provisions, or more effective techniques, they bring into play a form of beneficent competition. On more than one occasion I have been present at a state legislative planning session and have heard the argument made that the state in question should liberalize its program because it was falling behind other states in its own economic bracket. This argument carried weight with legislative committees. The stimulating effect of competition is at least as real as the deterrent effect of competition. This might be called the Commons effect, after John R. Commons, who relied on such competition to achieve many of his social goals. In the Commons formula, you induced a few leaders (firms or states) to step out in front with the expectation that others would follow. Such a gradual, tested kind of growth is likely to prove sound—proceeding not by large erratic jumps that may need to be retraced, but by smaller, steadier steps that result in durable advances.

Also, there may well be other periods like the present, when the mood of Congress is to delimit and restrict. In a national system, such moods affect all states, whether particular states share the mood or not. There is still much truth in Samuel Gompers's dictum: "What the government gives, the government can take away."

Cost Sharing. Some states may have failed in liberality not because they were unwilling to do better but because they were unable. The burden of providing adequate unemployment benefits was greater than their limited resources could sustain. For this situation, one solution often proposed, from the earliest years of the program to the recommendations of the NCUC, has been some form of cost sharing among the states. The proposals amount to saying that employers in

132

some states should receive financial aid from their more fortunate fellows.

The evidence justifying use of the word "should" is usually not even identified, let alone developed. Presumably the strongest evidence would be found in states having three characteristics: (1) the state is carrying an unusually heavy burden (its unemployment rate is above average); (2) the state is lacking in financial resources (its per capita income is below average); and (3) for these two reasons it fails to provide adequate benefits (its program is below average in liberality).

Only five states exhibit these three characteristics: Arkansas, Idaho, Maine, New Mexico, and West Virginia. Between them they account for 2.7 percent of all covered employment, and only Maine had an unemployment rate notably above the average and was thus likely to have received any significant amount of help from any cost-sharing program that might have been in existence during the decade surveyed by tables 7 and 22. All the other states are either above average in liberality or below average in unemployment or above average in per capita income.

Another argument used to bolster proposals for cost sharing is drawn from general economic considerations. A state is said to be not "responsible" for its higher than average unemployment because the unemployment is inseparable from the kinds of industries that characterize the state. Still, in a market economy, firms are responsible for all regular costs of doing business, whether the costs are avoidable or not. Although it is true that the people in Texas who wish to have the use of automobiles manufactured in Michigan must be ready to share in the cost of the unemployment benefits necessarily connected with production, it does not follow that the best way to achieve this sharing is by having the employers of Texas pay a subsidy to the employers of Michigan. Normally the purchasers of automobiles find the cost included in the price they have to pay for automobiles; this is how the market usually allocates resources.

Employer Responsibility

Of the two original choices made in allocating unemployment insurance costs—between states and between employers—the second is probably the more significant. If we had chosen to have a single national system, with a common pocketbook for the whole country, but had chosen to experience-rate the system, our allocation of costs among the states would have been quite similar to the actual allocation.

As explained in chapter 4, the states have been free to adopt as little or as much experience rating as they wished. Thus the degree of experience rating operative in the system accurately reflects individual choices freely made by the states. Presumably the states have chosen to actualize the potential of experience rating to the extent they have because they judged the effects of experience rating to be beneficial. I have the impression, gained from years of working with the various states, that they were mainly influenced by two of experience rating's effects—those on the allocation of costs and on the administration of the program. That is, the states generally have been in sympathy with Edwin Witte's early statement: "In a socialistic economy it might be proper to have all industry collectively bear the costs of unemployment; in a private economy, where the profits go to particular entrepreneurs, all costs of production should be borne by the particular establishment."[2] Also, the states have experienced how dependent they are on employer cooperation in the administration of the program and how difficult it is to get cooperation without the financial incentive provided by experience rating.

The desirable effects of experience rating could be enhanced by increasing the degree of experience rating—chiefly by decreasing the amount of noncharging and increasing the maximum tax rate. To judge from the maximum tax rates that employers have long been paying in workmen's compensation, the maximum rate in unemployment insurance could safely be increased in most states. The increase could be achieved without serious economic dislocation if it were announced well in advance and brought into operation only gradually, by steps, over a period of years. Experience rating will also be stronger if its rates are allowed to descend to zero. The necessary socialized costs can be financed through a special common tax, as a dozen states now do.

The NCUC held hearings on a number of proposals to change experience rating and reported the results as follows:

> Most respondents favor experience rating as it in fact now exists, including the prerogative of States to select the specific formula to be utilized in the State. With respect to any further involvement by the secretary of Labor or a three-person panel, there is overwhelming opposition. This indicates that most respondents feel that the present system of State discretion should not be supplemented in any way.[3]

[2] Robert J. Lampman, ed., *Social Security Perspectives: Essays by Edwin E. Witte* (Madison: University of Wisconsin Press, 1962), p. 275.

[3] National Commission on Unemployment Compensation, *Basic Structure of a Federal-State Unemployment Insurance Program and Related Supporting Provisions, Responses to the National Commission on Unemployment Compensation*, November 1979, p. 10.

Unemployment Benefits American Style

This review of state experience has produced some specific recommendations that are scattered through the text, but its chief concern has been not with specifics but with the very general question whether our choices in unemployment insurance should continue to be guided by the value of individual responsibility or should begin to reflect more social sharing. In 1944 Evelyn M. Burns presented to the American Economic Association a paper in which she delineated a possible evolutionary law of growth underlying all social security programs, including unemployment insurance. In her paper, Professor Burns identified three stages of social insurance evolution. The stages differed from one another in a number of ways, but in general each succeeding stage emphasized individual responsibility less and social responsibility more. Professor Burns placed the United States of that period in Stage 2 and judged that we were in movement toward Stage 3. Twenty years later, in 1964, the same author discussed the same theme before the Industrial Relations Research Association and reported that the United States had not yet arrived at Stage 3. In discussing Burns's paper, Professor Margaret Gordon noted an anomaly: Although significant movement had occurred toward Stage 3 in other social security programs, relatively little movement in this direction had occurred in unemployment insurance.

Until the present, the distinctive characteristic of unemployment insurance in the United States can be summed up, I believe, in the statement that unemployment benefits are seen as an extension of the wage system. To the extent that this is true, unemployment insurance has all the disadvantages of the wage system. It does not, for example, closely fit benefits to proved individual need. At best it approximates average presumed need. Neither does it attempt to alter the worker, by retraining or relocating him, to improve his job prospects. At best it maintains his income for a time while he finds a job for himself.

On the other hand, unemployment insurance has all the advantages of the wage system. The unemployed claim their benefits with a sense of dignity and freedom that attaches to an earned reward. President Roosevelt insisted from the beginning that the proposed system should have this characteristic, and in so doing he accurately reflected the temper of the American people. As a result, unemployment benefits in this country are less liable to the fate that overtook the Russian system. When the Communist government came into power, it immediately abolished unemployment insurance. The reason given was, of course, that in a socialist society there is no unemployment. Still, the Communist definition meant that a waitress in a resort hotel was not considered unemployed during the winter as long as there were snow-shoveling jobs in Moscow—nor was an engineer considered unemployed between jobs when there were ditch-digging jobs available. I was told of these two examples, among others, by an American official who went to Russia on an exchange program and diligently investigated how Russia managed without having a program of unemployment benefits.

Although the vertical lines of figure 1 still seem to describe the values pertinent to unemployment insurance in the United States today, there are pressures to modify them. The pressures take the form of proposals to link unemployment insurance with other programs and stem from the two disadvantages of the unemployment insurance program mentioned above. One pressure comes from those involved in the war on poverty. There have been many proposals to modify the provisions of unemployment insurance so as to perform some of the functions that would otherwise have to be performed by welfare programs. There is also pressure from the side of the new manpower programs. The grand strategy of manpower planning calls on unemployment insurance to attempt more than mere income maintainance for the job seeker.

In my judgment, unemployment insurance would be wise to avoid this Scylla and Charybdis—to keep its skirts clear of the welfare programs and to discourage the enthusiastic embrace of the manpower programs. That conclusion is based on two characteristics of the unemployment insurance program, its distinctive clientele and its high degree of success. The clientele of the unemployment insurance system is a uniquely significant group that should not be lumped with other groups but should be kept in a distinct program where it can be handled according to its own specific character. The clientele of unemployment insurance consists of the core of the labor force, the regularly employed. In modern society, the regular members of the labor force are a crucial social group. Economically, the prosperity of the country depends upon how effectively this group functions. Politically, the stability of the country turns on how satisfied this group is. There is nothing that can bring down a government faster than dissatisfaction among this group.

This distinctive group differs from the clientele of the other social security programs by being more closely intertwined in the competitive market process. Unemployment insurance pays benefits to potential workers—rather than to widows, children, the aged, the sick, the disabled, the retired, and all others normally unable to support themselves by the work they do. Where the other social security programs operate like Red Cross units behind the lines, unemployment insurance operates somewhat like a troop unit at the front and has implications for the general economic issues of wages, industrial discipline, productivity, unemployment, and inflation. A symbol of this market character of unemployment insurance is to be seen in the fact that unemployment insurance is not administered by the Department of Health and Human Services, as are the other social security programs, but by the Department of Labor. Unemployment benefits are inescapably related to the competitive market.

The second characteristic of unemployment insurance is simply its success. Unemployment insurance is an immense program that has been immensely successful. Not completely successful, of course, but as public programs go, it has had an admirable track record. It would be difficult to find another public program that has performed better. Neither the welfare programs to the left of unemployment insurance nor the manpower programs to the right can compare with unemployment insurance in point of success. Granted, unemployment insurance has a simpler and easier task than the other social programs, but that in itself is an additional reason for limiting unemployment insurance to the performance of its own proper function.

For forty years, unemployment insurance has slowly but steadily grown in size and strength. The slowness has probably been more of an advantage than a disadvantage because it has meant caution. The program has never had to reverse itself. Each expansion has been successfully assimilated and has become the foundation for another advance. As compared with its companions in the social security system—the old-age programs and the various welfare programs—unemployment insurance looks reassuringly sound and healthy.

That may be said despite the current financial problems of the system. The system's present situation is partly the result of an unusually severe recession. Still, recessions are temporary phenomena, and we can plausibly expect the system to work its way back from this recession as it has done before. I recall the hand-wringing that accompanied the recessions of 1954 and 1958 and the predictions that the state system was doomed, but the system recovered very nicely from those recessions. If the present unemployment insurance system is relieved of the burden of Federal Supplemental Benefits and perhaps part of that involving extended benefits, I would expect the state programs gradually to regain their health. Their present problems are also a legacy of our recent attempt to use the program to achieve ends for which it was not intended. If an efficient screwdriver is used as a crowbar, we should not be surprised when the screwdriver becomes somewhat bent.

We have a program with a solid history of success in caring for a uniquely important clientele. It would seem the better part of wisdom to leave this program essentially unchanged, free to continue to care for the regular members of the labor force with almost automatic effectiveness. The key to maintaining the present successful program is to maintain the present financing system, which has made unemployment benefits "a regular cost of doing business." From this characteristic have stemmed all the most distinctive qualities of unemployment insurance in the United States. The moral of this review of forty-five years of experience might be put in a sentence: *Maintain the character of unemployment insurance as an extension of the wage system by continuing to make unemployment insurance a regular cost of doing business.*

Appendix

TABLE 17
BENEFITS, TAXES, AND RESERVES AS A PERCENTAGE OF TOTAL WAGES: TWENTY-THREE DEBTOR STATES, AVERAGES FOR SELECTED PERIODS, 1957–1976

	1957–62	1963–69	1970–76	1957–76
U.S. total				
Benefits	1.44	0.80	1.28	1.17
Taxes	1.10	1.03	0.88	1.00
Reserves	3.67	3.33	1.97	2.99
Alabama				
Benefits	1.33	0.64	1.05	1.01
Taxes	0.98	0.95	0.65	0.86
Reserves	3.09	3.10	1.54	2.58
Arkansas				
Benefits	1.39	0.82	1.20	1.14
Taxes	0.97	0.95	0.87	0.93
Reserves	4.34	2.54	1.39	2.76
Connecticut				
Benefits	1.59	0.80	2.17	1.51
Taxes	1.46	1.01	1.17	1.21
Reserves	4.95	4.20	−0.27	2.96
Delaware				
Benefits	1.19	0.67	1.25	1.04
Taxes	0.99	0.78	0.90	0.89
Reserves	1.71	2.30	1.17	1.73
District of Columbia				
Benefits	0.54	0.52	1.10	0.72
Taxes	0.52	0.45	0.53	0.50
Reserves	5.69	3.95	1.45	3.70

(Table continues)

139

TABLE 17 (continued)

	1957–62	1963–69	1970–76	1957–76
Florida				
Benefits	0.79	0.37	0.93	0.70
Taxes	0.84	0.58	0.46	0.63
Reserves	2.79	3.09	1.60	2.49
Hawaii				
Benefits	1.02	0.97	1.43	1.14
Taxes	0.79	1.22	1.33	1.11
Reserves	4.48	2.93	1.20	2.87
Illinois				
Benefits	1.08	0.52	1.03	0.88
Taxes	0.87	0.53	0.60	0.67
Reserves	2.76	2.64	0.70	2.03
Maine				
Benefits	1.82	0.87	1.73	1.47
Taxes	1.21	1.02	1.30	1.18
Reserves	4.35	3.63	1.21	3.05
Maryland				
Benefits	1.59	0.67	1.07	1.11
Taxes	1.35	1.03	0.60	0.99
Reserves	2.79	4.04	1.60	2.81
Massachusetts				
Benefits	1.64	1.18	2.03	1.63
Taxes	1.21	1.39	1.47	1.36
Reserves	3.63	3.02	2.34	3.00
Michigan				
Benefits	1.86	0.61	1.63	1.37
Taxes	1.42	1.09	1.06	1.19
Reserves	2.21	3.35	0.98	2.18
Minnesota				
Benefits	1.19	0.62	1.37	1.06
Taxes	0.68	0.78	0.79	0.75
Reserves	2.28	1.15	0.77	1.40
Montana				
Benefits	2.18	0.99	1.32	1.50
Taxes	1.12	0.92	0.94	0.99
Reserves	6.45	3.56	1.89	3.97

TABLE 17 (continued)

	1957–62	1963–69	1970–76	1957–76
Nevada				
Benefits	1.67	1.19	1.68	1.51
Taxes	1.53	1.36	1.34	1.41
Reserves	4.60	3.63	1.57	3.27
New Jersey				
Benefits	1.82	1.21	2.12	1.72
Taxes	1.38	1.26	1.45	1.36
Reserves	3.48	3.20	0.34	2.34
New York				
Benefits	1.60	1.03	1.54	1.39
Taxes	1.32	1.21	1.05	1.19
Reserves	4.33	4.13	2.18	3.55
Ohio				
Benefits	1.52	0.50	0.92	0.98
Taxes	0.75	0.90	0.57	0.74
Reserves	2.74	2.45	2.06	2.42
Oregon				
Benefits	1.85	0.94	1.41	1.40
Taxes	1.75	1.25	1.11	1.37
Reserves	2.43	3.93	1.94	2.77
Pennsylvania				
Benefits	2.09	0.78	1.61	1.49
Taxes	1.58	1.43	0.95	1.32
Reserves	1.34	2.72	2.19	2.08
Rhode Island				
Benefits	2.01	1.13	2.45	1.86
Taxes	2.02	1.53	1.54	1.70
Reserves	3.40	4.70	1.11	3.07
Vermont				
Benefits	1.50	1.06	1.84	1.47
Taxes	0.95	1.37	0.94	1.09
Reserves	4.80	3.07	0.18	2.68
Washington				
Benefits	1.73	1.06	2.34	1.71
Taxes	1.55	1.23	1.47	1.42
Reserves	6.62	5.48	0.48	4.19

NOTE: Benefits include the state's share of extended benefits. Puerto Rico and the Virgin Islands were omitted because the data are not complete.

SOURCE: U.S. Department of Labor, *Handbook of Unemployment Insurance Financial Data, 1938-1970*, and relevant *Program Letters, 1971-1976*.

TABLE 18

Benefits, Taxes, Reserves, and Taxable Wage Base for Eight Debtor States, 1957–1976

State	1957	1958	1959	1960	1961	1962	1963	1964	1965
United States total									
Benefits	1.00	2.05	1.22	1.40	1.72	1.26	1.24	1.05	0.84
Taxes	0.89	0.86	1.05	1.17	1.23	1.39	1.35	1.27	1.18
Reserves	4.99	4.05	3.57	3.29	2.80	2.84	2.88	2.96	3.24
Wage base	3,000								
Vermont									
Benefits	1.10	1.93	1.03	1.35	2.12	1.45	1.78	1.66	1.04
Taxes	1.01	0.86	0.87	0.89	1.01	1.07	1.12	1.27	1.45
Reserves	6.60	5.85	5.20	4.53	3.57	3.04	2.35	1.88	2.13
Wage base	3,000							3,600	
Rhode Island									
Benefits	2.26	2.87	1.72	1.72	1.98	1.53	1.66	1.30	0.97
Taxes	2.14	2.07	2.03	2.02	1.94	1.92	1.87	1.81	1.77
Reserves	3.61	3.00	3.15	3.41	3.39	3.68	3.88	4.06	4.54
Wage base	3,600								
Connecticut									
Benefits	0.93	2.82	1.51	1.47	1.81	1.01	1.06	1.02	0.71
Taxes	0.78	0.74	1.04	1.23	1.20	1.18	1.14	1.10	1.08
Reserves	7.15	5.55	4.79	4.49	3.87	3.87	3.87	3.86	4.12
Wage base	3,000								
Pennsylvania									
Benefits	1.46	3.02	1.95	1.90	2.47	1.74	1.58	1.10	0.69
Taxes	1.07	1.23	1.64	1.79	1.88	1.89	1.79	1.83	1.78
Reserves	2.59	0.99	1.35	1.25	0.83	1.03	1.05	1.49	2.30
Wage base	3,000							3,600	
New Jersey									
Benefits	1.71	2.62	1.63	1.61	1.78	1.59	1.73	1.52	1.17
Taxes	1.24	1.31	1.32	1.41	1.48	1.51	1.43	1.34	1.30
Reserves	6.10	5.03	4.43	4.13	3.75	3.53	3.21	2.95	2.98
Wage base	3,000								
Illinois									
Benefits	0.61	1.70	0.94	0.96	1.29	0.97	0.94	0.69	0.49
Taxes	0.64	0.50	0.61	1.12	1.14	1.19	1.09	0.99	0.70
Reserves	3.83	2.83	2.34	2.52	2.42	2.59	2.73	2.93	3.01
Wage base	3,000								

1966	1967	1968	1969	1970	1971	1972	1973	1974	1975	1976
0.62	0.69	0.61	0.58	1.01	1.23	1.03	0.80	1.12	2.03	1.56
1.07	0.89	0.77	0.70	0.65	0.65	0.85	0.98	0.94	0.90	1.16
3.46	3.54	3.54	3.46	3.11	2.41	2.06	2.13	1.88	0.80	1.35
						4,200				
0.67	0.79	0.78	0.69	1.16	1.93	1.69	1.41	1.86	3.18	2.20
1.89	1.61	1.22	1.01	0.85	0.59	0.61	1.07	1.20	1.15	1.13
3.15	3.80	4.06	4.12	3.72	2.22	0.73	0.34	2.07	−2.53	−3.32
						4,200				
0.89	0.98	1.03	1.09	1.75	2.30	1.85	1.81	2.29	3.85	2.27
1.46	1.38	1.24	1.18	1.05	1.01	1.28	1.56	1.55	1.98	2.11
4.82	5.06	5.13	5.10	4.34	2.84	1.98	1.54	0.61	−1.76	−2.08
						4,200			4,800	
0.46	0.61	0.84	0.87	1.75	2.88	1.98	1.28	1.64	2.92	2.18
1.04	0.89	0.93	0.87	0.88	0.79	1.13	1.25	1.25	1.38	1.51
4.44	4.59	4.46	4.04	3.38	0.91	−0.11	−0.14	−0.51	−2.27	−3.13
		3,600				4,200			6,000	
0.46	0.56	0.56	0.51	0.88	1.18	1.37	1.12	1.39	3.04	2.23
1.62	1.42	0.83	0.72	0.66	0.69	0.77	1.04	1.14	1.18	1.20
2.86	3.72	3.86	3.74	3.53	2.97	2.11	1.94	1.58	3.04	0.16
						4,200				
0.91	0.97	1.10	1.07	1.49	1.95	1.89	1.55	1.97	2.89	2.16
1.26	1.18	1.19	1.14	1.13	1.09	1.23	1.64	1.60	1.67	1.77
3.20	3.44	3.41	3.21	2.76	1.49	0.73	0.75	0.18	−1.54	−1.98
		3,600				4,200			4,800	5,400
0.35	0.43	0.41	0.36	0.69	0.86	0.77	0.54	0.68	1.78	1.69
0.42	0.22	0.13	0.18	0.22	0.34	0.66	1.00	0.85	0.46	0.72
2.90	2.65	2.28	2.01	1.55	1.03	0.85	1.29	1.40	−0.08	−1.23
						4,200				

(Table continues)

TABLE 18 (continued)

State	1957	1958	1959	1960	1961	1962	1963	1964	1965
Delaware									
Benefits	0.90	1.53	1.07	1.01	1.49	1.14	0.90	0.89	0.54
Taxes	0.45	0.40	1.02	1.48	1.21	1.40	1.33	1.21	0.99
Reserves	2.48	1.41	1.32	1.79	1.53	1.75	2.11	2.36	2.63
Wage base	3,600								
Michigan									
Benefits	1.36	3.75	1.38	1.46	2.20	1.09	0.81	0.63	0.42
Taxes	1.19	1.23	1.42	1.58	1.54	1.53	1.63	1.50	1.22
Reserves	3.04	2.26	2.12	2.18	1.66	1.98	2.69	3.32	3.66
Wage base	3,000						3,600		

NOTE: Benefits, taxes, and reserves are shown as a percentage of total wages. Benefits are inclusive of the states' share of extended benefits. Debtor states are those whose debts as of December 31, 1978, equaled at least 1.5 percent of their respective total covered payrolls.

1966	1967	1968	1969	1970	1971	1972	1973	1974	1975	1976
0.58	0.69	0.54	0.53	0.81	0.89	0.68	0.58	1.29	2.46	1.73
0.61	0.49	0.43	0.42	0.57	0.71	1.04	1.17	0.99	0.87	0.97
2.54	2.36	2.14	1.97	1.72	1.47	1.75	2.29	1.85	−0.02	−0.86
						4,200				
0.49	0.76	0.62	0.56	1.43	1.40	1.04	0.68	1.65	3.06	1.52
1.13	0.83	0.65	0.65	0.61	0.63	1.31	1.25	1.07	1.04	1.47
3.81	3.64	3.20	3.15	2.49	1.48	1.62	2.10	1.42	−1.05	−1.22
						4,200				5,400

SOURCE: U.S. Department of Labor, *Handbook of Unemployment Insurance Financial Data, 1938-1970,* and relevant *Program Letters, 1971-1976.*

TABLE 19

ADVANCES TO STATES FROM THE FEDERAL UNEMPLOYMENT ACCOUNT AND REPAYMENTS, 1972–1978

($ millions)

	1972	1973	1974	1975	1976	1977	1978	Repayments	Total Outstanding[a]
Alabama				10.0	20.0	26.7		29.7	27.0
Arkansas					20.0	10.0		10.5	19.5
Connecticut	31.8	21.7	8.5	203.0	137.0	75.0	37.0	103.5	410.5
Delaware				6.5	14.0	16.1	10.4		47.0
District of Columbia				7.0	26.6	25.4	8.4	2.9	64.5
Florida					10.0	32.0		42.0	0
Hawaii					22.5			22.5	0
Illinois				68.8	446.5	243.3	187.9		946.5
Maine				2.4	12.5	8.0	13.5		36.4
Maryland					36.1	26.5		62.6	0

State									Total[a]
Massachusetts				140.0	125.0				265.0
Michigan				326.0	245.0	53.0			624.0
Minnesota				47.0	76.0	49.0			172.0
Montana					1.4	7.9	1.2		10.5
Nevada								7.6	0
New Jersey				352.2	145.0	141.7	96.0	40.0	694.9
New York						155.8	180.0		335.8
Ohio								1.9	0
Oregon								18.5	0
Pennsylvania				173.8	379.1	373.3	261.0		1,187.2
Puerto Rico				35.0	22.0	18.2	13.5		88.7
Rhode Island				45.8	20.0	9.0	31.0	3.7	102.1
Vermont	5.3			23.0	9.2	10.3		1.4	46.4
Virgin Islands				2.5	5.6	2.8			10.9
Washington		40.7	3.4	50.0	55.3			149.4	0
Total	31.8	62.4	17.2	1,493.0	1,854.9	1,285.9	839.9	496.2	5,088.9

[a] As of December 31, 1978.

SOURCE: U.S. Department of Labor.

TABLE 20

Estimated Difference in Size of Debt in 1978 If State's Reserve Had Been Adequate in 1969
($ millions)

| | Reserves at End of 1969 | | | Debt at End of 1978 | |
| | Actual | Adequate[a] | Difference (2) minus (1) | Actual | Estimated difference (4) minus (3) |
State	(1)	(2)	(3)	(4)	(5)
Arkansas	52.7	54.1	1.3	19.5	18.2
Connecticut	304.7	324.6	19.9	410.5	390.6
Delaware	24.2	29.6	5.3	47.0	41.7
Illinois	499.7	642.6	142.8	946.5	803.7
Maine	44.5	54.3	9.8	36.4	26.6
Michigan	630.3	1,108.0	477.7	624.0	146.3
Minnesota	120.3	163.5	43.1	172.0	128.9
Montana	25.7	33.1	7.5	10.5	3.0
New Jersey	482.7	593.6	110.9	694.9	584.0
Pennsylvania	863.9	1,046.0	182.1	1,187.2	1,005.1
Total	3,048.7	4,049.4	1,000.4	4,148.5	3,148.1

[a] Adequate reserve: a reserve ratio equal to 1.5 times the highest previous twelve-month benefit-cost rate.

Source: U.S. Department of Labor, Unemployment Insurance Service.

TABLE 21
INSURED UNEMPLOYMENT RATE FOR UNITED STATES AND FOR EIGHT STATES WITH LARGEST DEBTS, 1951–1976

Year	U.S. Total	Vt.	R.I.	Conn.	Pa.	N.J.	Ill.	Del.	Mich.
1951	2.7	2.4	7.2	1.9	2.4	3.1	2.7	1.1	2.6
1952	2.8	3.9	6.6	1.8	3.2	3.1	2.5	1.0	3.1
1953	2.7	2.2	4.9	1.3	3.0	3.1	2.1	1.2	2.1
1954	5.2	5.5	9.6	4.2	7.2	5.8	5.3	3.1	6.5
1955	3.4	4.6	5.5	3.0	4.9	4.5	3.0	1.8	2.7
1956	3.1	2.5	4.9	2.2	4.3	4.4	2.2	1.6	5.3
Average 1951–1956	3.3	3.5	6.5	2.4	4.2	4.0	3.0	1.6	3.7
1957	3.6	3.9	7.0	3.2	5.0	5.2	2.5	2.4	4.8
1958	6.5	6.5	8.6	7.3	9.6	7.8	5.4	4.2	12.2
1959	4.2	3.9	5.3	4.3	6.7	5.3	3.2	3.3	5.0
1960	4.7	4.6	5.4	4.6	6.6	5.4	3.4	3.1	5.3
1961	5.7	6.3	6.2	5.1	8.1	6.0	4.3	4.3	7.8
1962	4.3	4.6	4.9	3.5	6.2	5.0	3.1	3.3	4.4
1963	4.2	5.8	5.5	3.6	5.8	5.3	3.1	2.6	3.5
Average 1957–1963	4.7	5.1	6.1	4.5	6.9	5.7	3.6	3.3	6.1
1964	3.7	4.8	4.7	3.4	4.2	4.8	2.4	2.6	2.7
1965	2.9	3.3	3.4	2.4	2.7	3.7	1.8	1.7	1.8
1966	2.2	2.2	2.7	1.5	1.9	3.0	1.2	1.6	1.7
1967	2.4	2.6	3.1	1.9	2.2	3.2	1.5	1.9	2.7
1968	2.2	2.4	3.2	2.4	2.0	3.2	1.5	1.6	2.4
1969	2.1	2.1	3.3	2.4	1.9	3.0	1.3	1.6	2.1
Average 1964–1969	2.6	2.9	3.4	2.3	2.5	3.5	1.6	1.8	2.2
1970	3.4	3.7	5.2	4.5	3.1	4.1	2.4	2.6	5.0
1971	4.1	5.6	6.0	6.2	4.2	5.5	3.1	2.7	5.3
1972	3.0	4.4	4.5	4.1	3.7	4.7	2.4	2.1	3.9
1973	2.5	3.8	4.3	3.0	3.1	4.3	1.8	1.9	2.8
1974	3.4	5.3	5.4	4.0	4.1	5.5	2.3	3.2	5.9
1975	6.1	8.2	9.7	7.0	7.6	8.1	5.8	5.5	8.8
1976	4.4	6.1	6.0	5.7	6.0	6.3	5.2	3.9	5.4
Average 1970–1976	3.8	5.3	5.9	4.9	4.5	5.5	3.3	3.1	5.3

NOTE: Insured unemployment is exclusive of claims for extended benefits and federal supplemental benefits. For the states' financial performance, see table 5.
SOURCE: U.S. Department of Labor, *Handbook of Unemployment Insurance Financial Data, 1938-1976.*

149

TABLE 22

Liberality Index: Ratio of Benefit-Cost Rate to Insured Unemployment Rate, by State and Year, 1968–1977

	1968	1969	1970	1971	1972	1973	1974	1975	1976	1977	Average, 1968–1977
United States											
B.C.R.	0.61	0.58	1.01	1.23	0.98	0.79	1.07	2.03	1.39	1.16	1.09
I.U.R.	2.20	2.10	3.40	4.10	3.00	2.50	3.40	6.10	4.40	3.70	3.49
L.I.	0.277	0.276	0.297	0.300	0.327	0.316	0.315	0.333	0.316	0.314	0.311
Alabama											
B.C.R.	0.62	0.47	0.76	0.90	0.72	0.54	0.78	1.99	1.32	1.12	0.92
I.U.R.	2.50	2.00	3.10	3.40	2.40	1.90	2.90	6.40	4.30	3.80	3.27
L.I.	0.248	0.235	0.245	0.265	0.300	0.284	0.269	0.311	0.307	0.295	0.282
Alaska											
B.C.R.	1.80	1.35	1.78	2.14	2.30	2.25	1.78	1.17	1.70	3.26	1.95
I.U.R.	7.70	6.70	8.30	9.20	8.00	7.50	6.60	5.90	7.60	11.00	7.85
L.I.	0.234	0.202	0.215	0.233	0.288	0.300	0.270	0.198	0.224	0.296	0.249
Arizona											
B.C.R.	0.52	0.32	0.58	0.63	0.44	0.41	0.87	2.20	1.24	0.72	0.79
I.U.R.	2.10	1.30	2.30	2.70	1.80	1.70	3.10	6.50	4.30	2.90	2.87
L.I.	0.248	0.246	0.252	0.233	0.244	0.241	0.281	0.339	0.288	0.248	0.279
Arkansas											
B.C.R.	0.69	0.63	0.99	0.96	0.69	0.65	0.86	2.47	1.30	1.04	1.03

I.U.R.	2.60	2.50	3.70	3.70	2.70	2.30	3.30	7.90	4.70	3.90	3.73
L.I.	0.265	0.252	0.268	0.260	0.256	0.283	0.261	0.313	0.277	0.267	0.276
California											
B.C.R.	1.10	1.03	1.58	1.72	1.27	1.12	1.41	2.12	1.54	1.26	1.42
I.U.R.	3.50	3.30	5.10	5.80	4.10	3.60	4.40	6.40	5.00	4.30	4.55
L.I.	0.314	0.312	0.310	0.297	0.310	0.311	0.321	0.331	0.308	0.293	0.311
Colorado											
B.C.R.	0.23	0.22	0.36	0.38	0.31	0.29	0.48	1.04	0.82	0.76	0.49
I.U.R.	0.80	0.70	1.30	1.40	1.10	1.00	1.60	3.30	2.70	2.50	1.64
L.I.	0.288	0.314	0.277	0.271	0.282	0.290	0.300	0.315	0.304	0.304	0.298
Connecticut											
B.C.R.	0.84	0.87	1.75	2.88	1.98	1.28	1.64	2.92	2.18	1.59	1.79
I.U.R.	2.40	2.40	4.50	6.20	4.10	3.00	4.00	7.00	5.70	4.30	4.36
L.I.	0.350	0.363	0.389	0.465	0.483	0.427	0.410	0.417	0.383	0.370	0.409
Delaware											
B.C.R.	0.54	0.53	0.81	0.89	0.68	0.58	1.29	2.46	1.73	1.39	1.09
I.U.R.	1.60	1.60	2.60	2.70	2.10	1.90	3.20	5.50	3.90	3.60	2.87
L.I.	0.338	0.331	0.312	0.330	0.324	0.305	0.403	0.447	0.444	0.386	0.380
District of Columbia											
B.C.R.	0.41	0.39	0.56	0.76	0.85	0.93	1.12	1.73	1.68	1.55	1.00
I.U.R.	1.40	1.20	1.80	1.90	1.90	1.90	2.30	3.80	3.40	3.30	2.29
L.I.	0.293	0.325	0.311	0.400	0.447	0.490	0.487	0.455	0.494	0.470	0.436

(Table continues)

151

TABLE 22 (continued)

	1968	1969	1970	1971	1972	1973	1974	1975	1976	1977	Average, 1968–1977
Florida											
B.C.R.	0.28	0.22	0.36	0.44	0.27	0.22	0.57	1.62	1.08	0.74	0.58
I.U.R.	1.50	1.20	1.90	2.40	1.40	1.20	2.20	4.50	3.80	2.80	2.29
L.I.	0.187	0.183	0.190	0.183	0.193	0.183	0.259	0.360	0.284	0.264	0.253
Georgia											
B.C.R.	0.28	0.22	0.44	0.47	0.31	0.30	0.65	1.88	1.02	0.78	0.64
I.U.R.	1.20	0.90	1.70	1.90	1.30	1.00	2.10	6.10	3.30	2.70	2.22
L.I.	0.233	0.244	0.259	0.247	0.239	0.300	0.310	0.308	0.309	0.289	0.286
Hawaii											
B.C.R.	0.67	0.55	0.97	1.76	1.65	1.38	1.66	2.03	2.34	1.68	1.47
I.U.R.	2.10	1.80	2.70	3.90	4.40	3.50	4.00	4.50	4.90	3.80	3.56
L.I.	0.319	0.306	0.359	0.451	0.375	0.394	0.415	0.451	0.478	0.442	0.413
Idaho											
B.C.R.	0.95	0.84	1.06	1.18	1.10	0.96	1.10	1.54	1.17	1.09	1.10
I.U.R.	3.30	3.00	3.90	4.30	3.60	3.20	3.80	5.30	4.40	3.90	3.87
L.I.	0.288	0.280	0.272	0.274	0.306	0.300	0.290	0.291	0.266	0.280	0.284
Illinois											
B.C.R.	0.41	0.36	0.69	0.85	0.77	0.54	0.68	1.78	1.69	1.43	0.92
I.U.R.	1.50	1.30	2.40	3.10	2.40	1.80	2.30	5.80	5.20	4.30	3.01
L.I.	0.273	0.277	0.288	0.274	0.321	0.300	0.296	0.307	0.325	0.333	0.306

Indiana											
B.C.R.	0.34	0.24	0.58	0.71	0.48	0.30	0.64	1.62	0.64	0.50	0.61
I.U.R.	1.40	1.00	2.60	3.00	1.80	1.20	2.30	5.40	2.40	2.00	2.31
L.I.	0.243	0.240	0.223	0.237	0.267	0.250	0.278	0.300	0.267	0.250	0.262
Iowa											
B.C.R.	0.40	0.46	0.75	0.86	0.63	0.50	0.52	1.41	1.25	1.06	0.78
I.U.R.	1.20	1.40	2.20	2.60	1.70	1.40	1.50	3.70	2.90	2.40	2.10
L.I.	0.333	0.329	0.341	0.331	0.371	0.357	0.347	0.381	0.431	0.442	0.373
Kansas											
B.C.R.	0.42	0.55	1.24	1.20	0.61	0.48	0.69	1.14	0.89	0.86	0.81
I.U.R.	1.30	1.60	3.60	3.70	1.90	1.50	2.00	3.40	2.60	2.40	2.40
L.I.	0.323	0.344	0.344	0.324	0.321	0.320	0.345	0.335	0.342	0.358	0.337
Kentucky											
B.C.R.	0.59	0.55	0.82	0.93	0.75	0.72	0.90	1.95	1.21	1.00	0.94
I.U.R.	2.30	2.10	3.10	3.50	2.40	2.10	2.80	6.20	4.00	3.40	3.19
L.I.	0.257	0.262	0.265	0.266	0.313	0.343	0.321	0.315	0.303	0.294	0.295
Louisiana											
B.C.R.	0.66	0.87	1.12	1.14	0.93	0.91	0.91	1.19	0.98	1.25	1.00
I.U.R.	2.30	2.80	3.90	3.80	2.80	2.80	2.90	4.10	3.50	3.60	3.25
L.I.	0.287	0.311	0.287	0.300	0.332	0.325	0.314	0.290	0.280	0.347	0.307
Maine											
B.C.R.	0.78	0.94	1.28	2.08	1.42	1.21	1.46	2.58	1.83	2.01	1.56
I.U.R.	2.80	3.60	4.70	6.80	4.60	3.90	5.00	8.20	6.00	5.70	5.13
L.I.	0.279	0.261	0.272	0.306	0.309	0.310	0.292	0.315	0.305	0.353	0.304

(Table continues)

153

TABLE 22 (continued)

	1968	1969	1970	1971	1972	1973	1974	1975	1976	1977	Average, 1968–1977
Maryland											
B.C.R.	0.55	0.47	0.76	1.13	0.97	0.65	0.80	1.80	1.17	1.05	0.94
I.U.R.	1.70	1.50	2.30	3.40	2.70	2.10	2.80	5.50	3.80	3.40	2.92
L.I.	0.324	0.313	0.330	0.332	0.359	0.310	0.286	0.327	0.308	0.309	0.322
Massachusetts											
B.C.R.	0.86	0.84	1.39	2.05	1.68	1.59	1.92	2.92	1.88	1.46	1.66
I.U.R.	2.80	2.80	4.40	5.70	4.50	4.30	5.30	8.10	5.50	4.30	4.77
L.I.	0.307	0.300	0.316	0.360	0.373	0.370	0.362	0.361	0.342	0.340	0.349
Michigan											
B.C.R.	0.62	0.56	1.43	1.40	1.04	0.68	1.65	3.06	1.52	1.11	1.31
I.U.R.	2.40	2.10	5.00	5.30	3.90	2.80	5.90	8.80	5.40	4.40	4.60
L.I.	0.258	0.267	0.286	0.264	0.267	0.243	0.280	0.348	0.282	0.252	0.285
Minnesota											
B.C.R.	0.46	0.36	0.78	0.98	0.87	0.76	1.03	1.67	1.38	1.10	0.94
I.U.R.	1.50	1.30	2.70	3.40	2.90	2.50	2.70	4.40	3.50	2.80	2.77
L.I.	0.307	0.277	0.289	0.288	0.300	0.304	0.382	0.380	0.394	0.393	0.339
Mississippi											
B.C.R.	0.42	0.41	0.60	0.55	0.32	0.32	0.45	1.44	0.74	0.72	0.60
I.U.R.	2.00	1.80	2.50	2.40	1.40	1.30	2.00	5.60	3.30	2.90	2.52
L.I.	0.210	0.228	0.240	0.229	0.229	0.246	0.225	0.257	0.224	0.248	0.237

	1	2	3	4	5	6	7	8	9	10	11
Missouri											
B.C.R.	0.45	0.48	0.84	0.94	0.71	0.60	0.79	1.79	1.07	0.86	0.85
I.U.R.	2.00	2.10	3.40	3.80	2.80	2.40	3.00	6.00	3.90	3.50	3.29
L.I.	0.225	0.229	0.247	0.247	0.254	0.250	0.263	0.298	0.274	0.246	0.259
Montana											
B.C.R.	0.77	0.75	1.00	1.07	1.14	1.09	1.26	1.81	1.56	1.52	1.19
I.U.R.	3.00	2.80	3.90	4.30	3.40	3.20	3.80	5.20	4.50	4.20	3.83
L.I.	0.257	0.268	0.256	0.249	0.335	0.341	0.332	0.348	0.347	0.362	0.313
Nebraska											
B.C.R.	0.39	0.34	0.51	0.66	0.53	0.52	0.66	1.37	0.81	0.58	0.64
I.U.R.	1.20	1.10	1.60	2.10	1.40	1.40	1.80	3.80	2.40	2.00	1.88
L.I.	0.325	0.309	0.319	0.314	0.379	0.371	0.367	0.361	0.338	0.290	0.339
Nevada											
B.C.R.	0.97	0.74	1.05	1.38	1.63	1.34	1.81	2.30	1.66	1.21	1.41
I.U.R.	3.50	2.70	3.70	4.70	4.60	3.70	5.00	6.40	5.10	3.80	4.32
L.I.	0.277	0.274	0.284	0.294	0.354	0.362	0.362	0.359	0.326	0.318	0.326
New Hampshire											
B.C.R.	0.20	0.24	0.62	1.11	0.64	0.47	0.97	2.41	1.03	0.68	0.84
I.U.R.	0.80	1.00	2.40	3.60	2.10	1.40	2.80	6.70	3.30	2.10	2.62
L.I.	0.250	0.240	0.258	0.308	0.305	0.336	0.346	0.360	0.312	0.324	0.320
New Jersey											
B.C.R.	1.10	1.07	1.49	1.95	1.89	1.55	1.97	2.89	2.16	1.90	1.80
I.U.R.	3.20	3.00	4.10	5.50	4.70	4.30	5.50	8.10	6.30	5.40	5.01
L.I.	0.344	0.357	0.363	0.355	0.402	0.361	0.358	0.357	0.343	0.352	0.359

(Table continues)

155

TABLE 22 (continued)

	1968	1969	1970	1971	1972	1973	1974	1975	1976	1977	Average, 1968–1977
New Mexico											
B.C.R.	0.72	0.56	1.01	1.02	0.82	0.86	1.01	1.30	0.99	0.76	0.91
I.U.R.	2.70	2.30	4.00	4.10	3.10	3.00	3.70	5.50	4.20	3.40	3.60
L.I.	0.267	0.244	0.253	0.249	0.265	0.287	0.273	0.236	0.236	0.224	0.251
New York											
B.C.R.	0.70	0.72	1.12	1.53	1.35	1.07	1.36	2.22	1.65	1.42	1.31
I.U.R.	2.50	2.50	3.80	4.60	4.20	3.50	4.40	7.00	5.60	4.90	4.30
L.I.	0.280	0.288	0.295	0.333	0.321	0.306	0.309	0.317	0.295	0.290	0.303
North Carolina											
B.C.R.	0.37	0.32	0.59	0.65	0.35	0.25	0.49	2.38	1.20	0.87	0.75
I.U.R.	1.60	1.40	2.30	2.40	1.40	1.00	2.20	7.10	3.50	2.80	2.57
L.I.	0.231	0.229	0.257	0.271	0.250	0.250	0.223	0.335	0.343	0.311	0.291
North Dakota											
B.C.R.	0.99	0.84	0.84	1.13	1.26	1.09	0.95	0.95	1.15	1.57	1.08
I.U.R.	2.90	2.80	3.00	3.80	3.10	2.70	2.80	2.90	3.30	3.80	3.11
L.I.	0.341	0.300	0.280	0.297	0.407	0.404	0.339	0.328	0.349	0.413	0.346
Ohio											
B.C.R.	0.30	0.27	0.59	0.83	0.58	0.36	0.73	1.96	1.04	0.91	0.76
I.U.R.	1.20	1.00	2.40	3.20	2.00	1.30	2.10	5.10	3.00	2.60	2.39
L.I.	0.250	0.270	0.246	0.259	0.290	0.277	0.348	0.384	0.347	0.350	0.317

State		C1	C2	C3	C4	C5	C6	C7	C8	C9	C10	C11
Oklahoma	B.C.R.	0.44	0.38	0.61	0.84	0.58	0.56	0.59	1.11	0.83	0.63	0.66
	I.U.R.	2.10	1.90	3.00	3.60	2.40	2.10	2.50	4.00	3.20	2.30	2.71
	L.I.	0.210	0.200	0.203	0.233	0.242	0.267	0.236	0.278	0.259	0.274	0.242
Oregon	B.C.R.	0.80	0.81	1.40	1.33	1.02	0.92	1.40	2.34	1.50	1.23	1.28
	I.U.R.	3.20	3.30	5.50	5.20	4.00	3.70	4.60	7.20	5.40	4.60	4.67
	L.I.	0.250	0.246	0.255	0.256	0.255	0.249	0.304	0.325	0.278	0.267	0.273
Pennsylvania	B.C.R.	0.56	0.51	0.88	1.18	1.37	1.12	1.39	2.86	2.23	2.00	1.41
	I.U.R.	2.00	1.90	3.10	4.20	3.70	3.10	4.10	7.60	6.00	5.60	4.13
	L.I.	0.280	0.268	0.284	0.281	0.370	0.361	0.339	0.376	0.372	0.357	0.341
Puerto Rico	B.C.R.	1.67	1.71	2.08	2.34	2.44	2.36	2.96	3.70	3.29	2.94	2.55
	I.U.R.	8.40	9.10	10.70	15.00	10.40	10.40	11.50	15.60	15.10	13.90	12.01
	L.I.	0.199	0.188	0.194	0.156	0.235	0.227	0.257	0.237	0.218	0.212	0.212
Rhode Island	B.C.R.	1.03	1.08	1.75	2.36	1.85	1.81	2.29	3.85	2.27	2.14	2.04
	I.U.R.	3.20	3.30	5.20	6.00	4.50	4.30	5.40	9.70	6.00	5.60	5.32
	L.I.	0.322	0.327	0.337	0.393	0.411	0.421	0.424	0.397	0.378	0.382	0.384
South Carolina	B.C.R.	0.44	0.41	0.71	0.79	0.45	0.34	0.66	2.66	1.18	0.88	0.85
	I.U.R.	1.70	1.50	2.60	2.80	1.70	1.20	2.50	7.80	3.70	2.80	2.83
	L.I.	0.259	0.273	0.273	0.282	0.265	0.283	0.264	0.341	0.319	0.314	0.287

(Table continues)

TABLE 22 (continued)

	1968	1969	1970	1971	1972	1973	1974	1975	1976	1977	Average, 1968–1977
South Dakota											
B.C.R.	0.37	0.36	0.45	0.52	0.47	0.45	0.49	0.95	0.77	0.76	0.56
I.U.R.	1.50	1.50	1.80	2.20	1.70	1.50	1.60	2.90	2.40	2.20	1.93
L.I.	0.247	0.240	0.250	0.236	0.277	0.300	0.306	0.328	0.321	0.346	0.290
Tennessee											
B.C.R.	0.55	0.54	0.85	0.84	0.55	0.45	0.71	1.89	1.06	0.87	0.83
I.U.R.	2.30	2.30	3.40	3.30	2.10	1.70	2.70	6.80	4.10	3.30	3.20
L.I.	0.239	0.235	0.250	0.255	0.262	0.265	0.263	0.278	0.259	0.264	0.260
Texas											
B.C.R.	0.18	0.18	0.35	0.43	0.35	0.26	0.27	0.54	0.34	0.30	0.32
I.U.R.	0.80	0.70	1.40	1.70	1.20	0.90	1.10	2.20	1.60	1.40	1.30
L.I.	0.225	0.257	0.250	0.253	0.292	0.289	0.246	0.246	0.213	0.214	0.246
Utah											
B.C.R.	0.85	0.76	0.90	0.99	0.96	0.87	0.87	1.57	1.15	0.96	0.99
I.U.R.	3.00	2.70	3.20	3.70	2.90	2.50	2.60	4.50	3.60	3.00	3.17
L.I.	0.283	0.282	0.281	0.268	0.331	0.348	0.335	0.349	0.319	0.320	0.312
Vermont											
B.C.R.	0.78	0.69	1.16	1.93	1.69	1.41	1.86	2.85	1.95	1.69	1.60
I.U.R.	2.40	2.10	3.70	5.60	4.40	3.80	5.30	8.20	6.10	5.00	4.66
L.I.	0.325	0.329	0.314	0.345	0.384	0.371	0.351	0.348	0.320	0.338	0.343

Virginia											
B.C.R.	0.16	0.15	0.27	0.34	0.20	0.18	0.30	1.23	0.70	0.65	0.42
I.U.R.	0.60	0.60	1.00	1.30	0.80	0.70	1.10	3.40	2.00	1.90	1.34
L.I.	0.267	0.250	0.270	0.262	0.250	0.257	0.273	0.362	0.350	0.342	0.312
Washington											
B.C.R.	0.69	0.84	2.92	3.45	2.04	1.64	1.76	2.11	1.71	1.34	1.85
I.U.R.	3.10	4.00	9.00	9.00	6.50	5.70	6.40	8.40	7.00	5.70	6.48
L.I.	0.223	0.210	0.324	0.383	0.314	0.288	0.275	0.251	0.244	0.235	0.286
West Virginia											
B.C.R.	0.62	0.50	0.59	0.72	0.76	0.68	0.74	1.31	0.93	0.99	0.78
I.U.R.	3.10	2.80	3.30	3.90	3.50	2.90	3.40	5.40	4.20	4.20	3.67
L.I.	0.200	0.179	0.179	0.185	0.217	0.234	0.218	0.243	0.221	0.236	0.214
Wisconsin											
B.C.R.	0.61	0.52	1.10	1.26	0.96	0.74	0.92	2.12	1.31	1.16	1.07
I.U.R.	2.00	1.70	3.50	3.90	3.00	2.10	2.70	5.70	3.90	3.20	3.17
L.I.	0.305	0.306	0.314	0.323	0.320	0.352	0.341	0.372	0.336	0.363	0.338
Wyoming											
B.C.R.	0.45	0.42	0.47	0.45	0.49	0.40	0.32	0.63	0.64	0.51	0.48
I.U.R.	1.50	1.30	1.60	1.90	1.50	1.30	1.20	2.10	1.80	1.50	1.57
L.I.	0.300	0.323	0.294	0.237	0.327	0.308	0.267	0.300	0.356	0.340	0.305

NOTE: B.C.R. = benefit-cost rate: benefits paid as a percentage of total wages. I.U.R. = insured unemployment rate: average insured unemployment as a percentage of covered employment. L.I. = liberality index: B.C.R. divided by I.U.R.

SOURCE: U.S. Department of Labor, *Handbook of Unemployment Insurance Financial Data, 1938–1977*.

TABLE 23

Eleven-Year Average Benefit-Cost Rates, Tax Rates, and Cost/Tax Ratios, Selected States, 1957–1967

Industry Division	Calif.[a]	Maine[a]	Mass.[b]	N.J.[c]	N.Y.[d]
All industry divisions					
Cost rate	2.7	2.0	2.4	—	2.5
Tax rate	2.6	—	2.2	—	2.5
Cost/tax ratio	105.1	—	106.2	99.3	98.8
Agriculture, forestry, and fisheries					
Cost rate	7.1	4.3	—	—	—
Tax rate	3.0	—	—	—	—
Cost/tax ratio	235.4	—	—	236.6	—
Mining, including quarrying					
Cost rate	2.3	5.4	—	—	—
Tax rate	2.6	—	—	—	—
Cost/tax ratio	86.7	—	—	104.0	—
Construction					
Cost rate	5.5	4.5	6.2	—	5.7
Tax rate	3.1	—	3.0	—	3.2
Cost/tax ratio	178.9	—	210.0	141.1	178.0
Manufacturing					
Cost rate	2.8	2.2	2.5	—	3.2
Tax rate	2.5	—	2.3	—	2.6
Cost/tax ratio	111.6	—	109.2	103.4	122.6
Transportation, communication, and utilities					
Cost rate	1.6	1.0	1.5	—	1.4
Tax rate	2.2	—	1.9	—	2.1
Cost/tax ratio	75.3	—	79.8	70.0	66.7
Wholesale and retail trade					
Cost rate	2.3	1.0	1.6	—	1.7
Tax rate	2.6	—	2.0	—	2.4
Cost/tax ratio	89.1	—	79.5	82.8	68.3

Ohio[b]	Oreg.[e]	Pa.	Utah[f]	Va.	Wash.[g]
1.8	1.7	2.4	1.0	0.7	2.1
1.7	2.0	2.7	1.0	0.9	2.4
106.9	87.2	88.4	108.3	77.5	86.6
5.6	—	—	—	1.8	8.6
2.4	—	—	—	1.4	2.5
232.8	—	—	—	124.3	347.9
2.9	—	6.7	1.0	1.6	3.1
2.0	2.2	3.1	0.8	1.4	2.4
148.3	105.1	212.8	120.2	108.4	129.5
5.5	3.2	5.3	2.8	1.2	3.7
2.9	2.4	3.4	1.4	1.5	2.5
189.7	132.8	159.1	203.6	77.5	146.9
1.9	2.1	2.6	0.9	0.8	2.2
1.8	2.1	2.9	0.8	0.9	2.4
105.3	102.6	88.5	110.8	83.7	91.6
1.0	0.8	1.2	0.4	0.3	1.5
1.1	1.7	2.3	0.8	0.6	2.4
86.9	49.0	53.2	56.4	44.9	61.5
1.1	1.1	1.6	0.8	0.3	1.7
1.5	1.9	2.5	1.0	0.7	2.4
76.3	58.7	64.7	84.0	49.6	71.0

(Table continues)

TABLE 23 (continued)

Industry Division	Calif.[a]	Maine[a]	Mass.[b]	N.J.[c]	N.Y.[d]
Finance, insurance, and real estate					
Cost rate	1.2	0.5	0.8	—	0.9
Tax rate	2.3	—	1.7	—	2.0
Cost/tax ratio	51.7	—	48.5	63.8	43.1
Services					
Cost rate	2.5	1.6	1.7	—	1.9
Tax rate	2.8	—	2.2	—	2.6
Cost/tax ratio	89.3	—	74.2	96.9	73.9

NOTE: Cost rate = benefit payments as percentage of taxable payrolls; tax rate = taxes as percentage of taxable payrolls; cost/tax ratio = benefit payments as percentage of taxes. Benefits include state-extended benefits paid in California; they exclude some $60 million of such benefits paid in Ohio in 1958-1959 and the relatively minor amount paid in New York in 1959. They do not include payments under the TUC and the TEUC programs. Tax rates include supplementary taxes not credited to employer reserves. No attempt was made to adjust tax rates for the increases in FUTA taxes resulting from TUC and TEUC programs.

[a] The Standard Industrial Classification Manual on which distributions by industry were based was revised in 1957, affecting the industrial distribution of benefits and taxes cited in this report. In the case of industrial *divisions*, it is believed that the revisions have not significantly affected the eleven-year averages. California departs from the SIC in two minor ways not significant for the purpose of the table. Maine data were adapted to include in the manufacturing division benefits chargeable to multi-industry establishments.

[b] Massachusetts and Ohio pay dependents' allowances; they are included in benefit costs and in the computation of the cost/tax ratio.

[c] The ratio shown for New Jersey is for the period from January 1, 1939 (when payments began in that state), through 1966; taxes paid before that date have been included in the calculation of the ratio. Excluded were benefit costs of and contributions paid by establishments that in June 1967 were no longer "active."

162

Ohio[b]	Oreg.[e]	Pa.	Utah[f]	Va.	Wash.[g]
0.6	0.6	0.8	0.5	0.2	1.2
1.1	1.8	2.1	0.9	0.6	2.4
52.2	34.0	35.7	54.3	30.8	48.5
1.2	1.3	1.8	1.1	0.3	1.7
1.7	2.0	2.5	1.2	0.8	2.4
72.7	64.4	69.6	95.7	43.7	70.3

[d] For New York, the rates shown for the service division include benefit costs and taxes relating to agriculture, forestry, and fishing; mining, including quarrying; and miscellaneous other establishments "not elsewhere classified."

[e] Data for Oregon cover the thirty-two-year period 1936 through 1967. Benefit payments began January 1, 1938; contributions before that date were included in the calculation of average tax rates and average cost/tax ratios.

[f] Data for Utah represent eight-year averages based on *total* wages for the years 1960 through 1967.

[g] Data for Washington based on benefits paid and cash contributions received during the years 1939 through 1967.

Sources: The data for benefit payments, taxable payrolls, and contributions, on which the rates shown in this table were based, were derived mainly from periodic and special reports issued by the employment security agencies of the respective states. In some cases where the data were not available in published form, they were supplied by the agency as requested.

TABLE 24

PERCENTAGE DISTRIBUTION OF TAXABLE WAGES OF ACTIVE ACCOUNTS
ELIGIBLE FOR EXPERIENCE RATING, BY TAX RATE,
RATE YEARS BEGINNING IN 1967

Type of Plan[a]	Taxable Wages ($ thousands)	0.0	0.1	0.2	0.3
Total, 51 states	144,265,674	2.6	6.9	3.7	5.5
Reserve-ratio plan	94,344,572	3.1	2.9	0.5	4.1
Arizona[b]	1,014,414				6.8
Arkansas[b]	941,610				33.7
California	15,246,979				
Colorado[b]	1,211,857	79.4			
District of Columbia[b]	818,447		53.2		
Georgia	2,775,501				8.7
Hawaii	601,219				
Idaho	403,147				
Indiana[b]	3,932,143		10.2		6.3
Iowa[b]	1,468,177	37.9	8.1	10.0	11.3
Kansas[b]	1,092,335	2.8		1.5	1.7
Kentucky[b]	1,492,084	29.3			
Louisiana	1,821,921				42.4
Maine[b]	593,445				
Massachusetts	5,449,307				
Michigan[b]	7,856,888	c	c	c	
Missouri[b]	3,037,190	15.8	35.3		18.6
Nebraska[b]	750,661		11.5	7.1	20.5
Nevada	421,464				
New Hampshire	509,691			29.5	
New Jersey[b]	5,107,115				
New Mexico	438,184		26.3		12.8
New York[b]	16,326,141				
North Carolina[b]	3,235,953				18.3
North Dakota[b]	211,909				
Ohio[b]	8,299,925		4.6	1.5	3.5
Rhode Island	789,264				
South Carolina[b]	1,514,319				
South Dakota[b]	217,576	53.0			
Tennessee	2,514,475				
West Virginia	1,109,321	13.1	12.8		7.4
Wisconsin[b]	3,141,910	6.0			8.0

Percentage Distribution by Employer Contribution Rate

0.4–0.5	0.6–0.9	1.0–1.8	1.9–2.6	2.7	2.71–3.1	3.2–3.5	3.6–3.9	4.0–4.4	4.5 and over
6.6	14.8	23.9	16.1	3.7	6.9	3.3	3.5	2.1	0.4
5.6	16.9	27.3	15.0	4.2	9.5	4.4	5.0	1.2	0.3
5.5	13.2	48.5	15.3	5.0	5.7				
12.9	17.2	15.6	7.1	0.7	4.9			8.0	
		8.1	38.6	7.4	15.9	9.0	21.0		
6.6				13.9					
15.0		18.4	2.6	10.8					
13.3	20.8	48.0	6.7	1.9	0.3	0.1	c	0.2	
	20.5	49.5	11.7		18.3				
	8.9	39.7	37.6	5.5	2.8	1.3	1.2	3.0	
11.2	20.7	37.5	3.9	0.5	9.8				
20.2	3.8	0.4	1.4	1.8	c	5.3			
11.6	27.9	38.3	4.3	11.9					
	30.9	11.8		20.0			8.0		
	21.2	12.4	2.4	21.6					
29.1	23.8	26.7	5.6	14.9					
	9.3	35.4	22.4	2.1	22.9	7.9			
13.3	18.4	49.7	6.7	2.1	1.3		1.6	3.6	3.2
	13.8	11.6		0.1			4.9		
29.5		14.0	2.5	14.9					
	15.1	38.1	26.8	20.0					
15.8	11.4	24.5	13.6		0.9	4.4			
	16.4	35.0	18.0		12.8		17.8		
	25.7	20.1	4.2	1.5	9.5				
	26.0	27.2	13.7	1.4	19.5	12.2			
14.2	23.6	20.4	13.0	6.2	0.8	0.6	0.6	0.4	2.0
		60.9	17.8	3.0	2.7	2.1	1.4	11.3	0.8
12.0	31.0	27.2	7.8		5.1	0.9	1.0	5.3	
		50.2	25.0	3.3	11.5	10.1			
	43.4	34.4	8.8	11.9	0.4	0.5	0.1	0.5	
20.5		16.2	2.3		0.8		7.1		
24.5	10.5	44.7	9.7	4.0	2.9	0.8	0.6	2.3	
6.3	3.7	14.4	19.0	23.2					
	23.6	40.6	8.9		2.9	1.8	1.7	6.6	

(Table continues)

TABLE 24 (continued)

Type of Plan[a]	Taxable Wages ($ thousands)	0.0	0.1	0.2	0.3
Benefit-wage-ratio plan	21,508,643		30.4	19.5	10.6
Alabama	1,865,170				
Delaware	499,716		26.2	27.7	6.7
Illinois	9,409,728		40.8	22.7	11.8
Oklahoma	1,254,291			57.9	
Texas	5,986,905		30.0	18.0	10.9
Virginia	2,492,833		31.0	4.7	19.7
Benefit-ratio plan	22,128,931	3.8	3.2	2.8	8.0
Florida	3,239,460	24.3[d]	19.5[d]	15.5	9.7
Maryland	2,352,332				57.3
Minnesota[b]	2,935,969				
Mississippi	943,762		8.3	13.4	11.4
Oregon	1,619,045				
Pennsylvania[b]	10,594,281				
Vermont	272,889				
Wyoming[b]	171,193	28.8			
Payroll-variation plan	3,303,305				
Alaska	279,592				
Utah	673,570				
Washington	2,350,143				
Other plans	2,980,223				
Connecticut[e]	2,646,267				
Montana[b,e]	333,956				

[a] States classified by type of plan in effect at end of 1967.
[b] Includes effects of voluntary contributions made toward credit for 1967 rates and of subsidiary and additional taxes where applicable.
[c] Less than 0.05 percent.
[d] In Florida the 24.3 percent consists of 13.5 percent with a 0 rate and 10.8 percent with rates of 0.01-0.04 percent; the 19.5 percent consists of 9.9 percent with rates

Percentage Distribution by Employer Contribution Rate

0.4–0.5	0.6–0.9	1.0–1.8	1.9–2.6	2.7	2.71–3.1	3.2–3.5	3.6–3.9	4.0–4.4	4.5 and over
16.9	9.3	7.9	2.3	2.5	0.4	c	c	0.1	
59.0	10.3	20.6	5.5	4.5					
6.9	8.6	7.1	2.7	1.8	12.3				
12.0	6.5	3.8	1.2	0.7	0.2	0.1	0.1	0.2	
6.0	13.3	12.3	3.6	6.9					
12.3	11.4	10.8	3.0	3.5					
22.5	12.4	5.0	1.9	3.0					
2.4	13.9	23.8	22.4	2.4	3.8	2.5	1.6	8.2	1.2
10.7	10.1	5.5	1.5	0.1	0.4	0.4	0.2	0.3	2.0
	16.7	12.8	5.1	1.1	6.6			0.4	
	73.5	12.7	2.8	1.5	0.7	0.8	0.6	0.8	6.5
20.2	21.2	13.9	4.5	7.0					
		50.0	40.1	9.9					
		31.4	37.1	2.1	5.8	4.3	2.8	16.5	
		26.9	26.8		8.8	17.8	9.1	10.6	
		42.8	10.2	2.4	2.9	12.9			
		18.5	76.1	0.3	0.8	1.7	1.6	1.0	
		19.6	19.6		9.8	19.5	19.4	12.1	
		82.5	17.4	0.1					
			99.6	0.4					
1.5	13.5	40.7	35.4	9.0					
	10.9	43.1	37.8	8.3					
13.0	34.6	21.4	16.5	14.6					

of 0.05-0.09 percent and 9.6 percent with a 0.10 percent rate.

c Connecticut has a compensable separations formula; Montana, a combination of benefit-contribution experience and payroll decline.

Source: Tabulation furnished by the Office of Actuarial and Research Service, Manpower Administration, U.S. Department of Labor.

TABLE 25

Significant Measures Relating to Negative-Balance Firms, Selected States, 1967 Rate Year

Measure	California	Massachusetts	Michigan	New Jersey	New York[a]	Ohio	South Carolina	Wisconsin
1. Number of firms with negative balances as a percentage of all firms	18.0	16.2	5.4	30.2	14.9	11.3	3.3	11.9
2. Taxable payrolls of firms with negative balances as a percentage of all taxable payrolls	14.2	11.8	3.6	20.4	13.8	4.4	3.7	8.5
3. Benefits charged to negative-balance firms as a percentage of benefits charged to all firms	51.8	55.3	34.8	—	61.6	34.2	24.7	60.8
4. Benefits charged to negative-balance firms as a percentage of their taxable payrolls	7.3	5.9	7.1	—	8.0	4.9	2.0	7.0

5. Deficit of negative-balance firms as a percentage of all benefits charged to all firms [b]	28.0	24.3	12.7	—	33.1	4.8	—	25.1
6. Deficit of negative-balance firms as a percentage of all benefits charged to negative-balance firms [b]	53.9	44.0	36.6	—	53.7	14.0	—	41.3
7. Deficit of negative-balance firms as a percentage of their taxable payrolls [b]	3.9	2.6	2.6	—	4.3	0.7	—	2.9
8. Average cost/tax ratios of negative-balance firms	217.1	178.6	157.6	—	216.0	116.3	—	170.4
9. Noncharged benefits as a percentage of all benefits paid	12.1	18.7	0.0	[c]	0.8	5.8	47.0	1.0

NOTE: Data are for active firms.

[a] New York data for all firms represent the sum of positive- and negative-balance firms.

[b] Deficit: excess of benefits charged to negative-balance firms over their contributions, including any subsidiary taxes.

[c] Less than 0.05 percent.

SOURCES: Form E.S.-204, Experience Rating Report for 1967 rate year; New York, *1967 Unemployment Insurance Tax Rates*, New York Division of Employment.

A NOTE ON THE BOOK

The typeface used for the text of this book is
Palatino, designed by Hermann Zapf.
The type was set by
Hendricks-Miller Typographic Company, of Washington, D.C.
Thomson-Shore, Inc., of Dexter, Michigan, printed
and bound the book, using Warren's Olde Style paper.
The cover and format were designed by Pat Taylor,
and the figures were drawn by Hördur Karlsson.
The manuscript was edited by Marcia Brubeck and
by Gertrude Kaplan, of the AEI Publications staff.

SELECTED AEI PUBLICATIONS

The AEI Economist, Herbert Stein, ed., published monthly (one year, $10; single copy, $1)

Money and Housing, John Charles Daly, mod. (31 pp., $3.75)

A Conversation with Dr. Ezra Sadan: Combating Inflation in Israel (18 pp., $2.25)

Achieving Financial Solvency in Social Security, Mickey D. Levy (61 pp., $3.75)

Experiences with Stopping Inflation, Leland B. Yeager (184 pp., paper $6.25, cloth $14.25)

The Congressional Budget Process after Five Years, Rudolph G. Penner, ed. (199 pp., paper $6.25, cloth $14.25)

Essays in Contemporary Economic Problems: Demand, Productivity, and Population, William Fellner, project director (350 pp., paper $9.25, cloth $17.25)

Health and Air Quality: Evaluating the Effects of Policy, Philip E. Graves and Ronald J. Krumm (156 pp., paper $6.25, cloth $14.25)

The Consumer Price Index: Issues and Alternatives, Phillip Cagan and Geoffrey H. Moore (69 pp., $4.25)

Prices subject to change without notice.

AEI ASSOCIATES PROGRAM

The American Enterprise Institute invites your participation in the competition of ideas through its AEI Associates Program. This program has two objectives:

The first is to broaden the distribution of AEI studies, conferences, forums, and reviews, and thereby to extend public familiarity with the issues. AEI Associates receive regular information on AEI research and programs, and they can order publications and cassettes at a savings.

The second objective is to increase the research activity of the American Enterprise Institute and the dissemination of its published materials to policy makers, the academic community, journalists, and others who help shape public attitudes. Your contribution, which in most cases is partly tax deductible, will help ensure that decision makers have the benefit of scholarly research on the practical options to be considered before programs are formulated. The issues studied by AEI include:

- Defense Policy
- Economic Policy
- Energy Policy
- Foreign Policy
- Government Regulation

- Health Policy
- Legal Policy
- Political and Social Processes
- Social Security and Retirement Policy
- Tax Policy

For more information, write to:

AMERICAN ENTERPRISE INSTITUTE
1150 Seventeenth Street, N.W.
Washington, D.C. 20036